KEEP THE
ORDERS
COMING

···

A POWERFUL GUIDE
TO MARKETING
YOUR BAKING BUSINESS

By Brette Hawks

Brette Hawks

@the.outofhome.baker

www.outofhomebaker.com

For
my husband Nate and
my two boys

who patiently waited for me
each evening as I wrote like a
mad woman before starting
dinner

TABLE OF CONTENTS

Preface: The Recipe for Success

If you wanted to make a delicious chocolate cake from scratch what's the first thing you would do?

Probably pull out that old family butter-stained index card with grandma's secret recipe, or look up your favorite cake blog to find their spin on a triple chocolate cake.

Either way, you're going to start with a recipe.

Because a recipe will tell you what ingredients you need and how to combine them in order to achieve maximum success with your final product- in this case, a chocolate cake.

As the expert baker that you are, it's probably pretty obvious that if you decide to leave out a few ingredients the results are going to be less than ideal. If you ditch a cup of flour, you're going to lose structure in your cake layers. If you nix the teaspoon of salt, the overall cake flavor is going to majorly suffer. All the ingredients work together in harmony to craft the perfect end result, and each of them plays an important role in achieving success. And if you ever do end up with a less-than-ideal cake result (hey, we've all been there!) then the first thing you're going to check to to see where you went wrong is the recipe.

Now as you're turning your love of baking into a business I have good news for you! Baking up a business from scratch is no different than making a chocolate cake: there's a recipe to follow. There are specific ingredients and steps that you need to follow if you want to see maximum success.

This recipe and it's ingredients are founded in solid business strategy that I studied as an undergrad student in the Food Science program at BYU. Food Science is nothing close to pastry school- it's vast science-based field all about the physical, chemical, and microbiological composition of food, and the production, safety, and quality management of food in it's many forms.

The Food Science major had two optional tracks for students: The technical track or the business track. As a young student in 2015, I remember looking at the treacherous course map for the technical track, packed with high level chemistry classes, and thought to myself, *Anything to avoid those classes...* So business track it was for me!

To my surprise and delight, I found that I thoroughly enjoyed my business classes! Everything from marketing and strategy, to entrepreneurship, to finance and accounting.

Throughout the business program, the ingredients of my recipe to success were woven into every class I took, although they were delivered in school through complex business models and foreign business jargon that could be difficult to decipher. Years later, I took all of those complex principles, added them on top of my own real business experience, and turned into a simple recipe that any home-based baker could understand, follow, and use to achieve success.

As I've coached thousands of bakers over the past few years, I've begun to notice a funny pattern amongst aspiring baker entrepreneurs. As attuned to the concept of a recipe that we are, most bakers unknowingly ignore most of the essential ingredients for success in business. They become hyper focused on the product, and naturally so- after all, that's usually what got us into this messy business stuff in the first place. The baking, the decorating, the creating, that love for creating in the kitchen. Crafting our cookies and perfecting our smooth buttercream cakes.

I watch bakers who should be having success struggle to grow their businesses because they don't extend their strategy beyond just tweaking the product. They add new flavors, new menu items, new designs. They constantly through out new products for sale without seeing a true increase in clientele, income, or success.

I speak from personal experience because that was me too!

If all you focus on in your business is the product, while it is a very important piece, you're not going to get as far as you want to. Remember, if all you put into your chocolate cake recipe is flour and nothing else, you're not going to get the most thrilling results.

The recipe for success in your baking business includes six key ingredients, of which your product is just one. There are five other crucial ingredients to account for and include as you're building up your business.

THE 6 INGREDIENT RECIPE FOR BAKING BUSINESS SUCCESS

MINDSET: THE FOUNDATION

To start off this recipe, everything is built on the foundation of your mindset. If I were to rattle off a few statements to you like "Think positive! Believe in yourself! Chase your dreams!" they would probably go in one ear and out the other as the biggest cliches you don't really care to hear. But the older I get, the more I realize that so many cliche statements actually consist of life's most valuable lessons. Lessons that everyone has heard, but very few actually master in daily living.

4

The mental ambiance you hold each day, the vibe you set in your own head, affects *everything* you do in business and in life.

Think of mindset like you would pre-heating your oven. You could make a recipe flawlessly, including every ingredient in precise amounts. But what good is it if the oven isn't on? An oven's heat is the catalyst for chemical and physical changes in batter. And your mindset is the catalyst for real growth and success in your business.

What exactly do I mean by mindset? Whether we realize it or not, we all walk around with a story that we tell ourselves, and that story becomes the basis for every decision we make. We form these internal stories all throughout our lives. We attach to and identify with the things others have told us, the experiences we had as kids, and events that we observe.

Take school for example. All of us went through grade school and we picked up a story. A default programming that still controls our decision making. We learned to memorize things so we could get the right answer. We learned to stay in line and jump through the hoops so we could fit in with the group. We learned to hide our greatest aspirations because they might not be acceptable in the system of society.

And we wonder why it's hard to step out of order to follow our passion and start a business. We've been subconsciously learning our whole lives that defying the system like that isn't safe!

Now, not every story we've picked up is negative. In school, I learned some amazing principles that I still hold dear. I was on my school's cross country team, and I learned how to work through pain, how to run your own race, how to learn from failed attempts and try again. Those lessons have been incredible strengths to me as I've started and grown my businesses.

From your family experiences growing up, you might of unknowingly picked up a story and belief system that money causes fights and divorce and it's better just to not talk about finances. You may have learned the value of hard work from your parents.

The fact of the matter is, all these stories we accumulate are neither truths nor falsehoods. They're just lenses of perception. Just a way we've learned to view the world. The beautiful fact of life is that ultimately you get to choose how you want to see things. You get to decide which stories you want to keep, which ones you want to dismiss, and which new ones you want to write. The one thing you have total and complete control over is your thoughts and what you decide to believe.

Resetting your mindset isn't about wallowing in what happened in the past. It's not about playing the blame game and being the victim. It is about bringing your awareness to the beliefs that you have, where they come from and then deciding whether you want to keep those beliefs or not.

Our thoughts act like rivers in a canyon. Slowly over time, the thoughts we choose to think and focus on carve out a grove in our brains. It soon becomes the path of least resistance. The same way a consistent flow of water created the incredible, deep fissures of the Grand Canyon, our thoughts, whether positive or negative, create paths in our mind where our thoughts will continue to naturally go, following the flow of what was carved before.

We carve these canyons in our mind from the stories, beliefs, and messages that we repeatedly tell ourselves. You might be stuck in an unconscious thought loop of "I'm not good enough. I'm falling behind. I'll never catch up," and whether or not it's true is negligible, because to your brain it becomes truth. And then you act based on that false truth, and thus is becomes your reality and reinforces that negative thought loop. It's a self-sabotaging, self-fulfilling cycle.

Once you realize what's happening in your mind and bring your attention to where your thoughts naturally flow, it then empowers you to change the direction of the current and carve out a new path of thought in your brain.

Easier said than done, right?

It takes daily effort and practice to pull your thoughts in a new direction. It doesn't happen just overnight. Elevating your mindset to a positive, optimistic, belief-prone state is a conscious, consistent exercise.

Think about a photographer. They have different lenses for their camera depending on what they want to focus on. Everyday, you have to choose which lens you want to use to see your business and your life. You decide where the focus is.

So how does this all tie into your baking business?

If you have a pre-set notion that things will be hard, they will be.

If you have a pre-determined belief that people don't pay for baked goods, they won't.

If you've already have it in your mind that you don't have the skills to succeed so why even try, you won't.

But if you change the lens, if you point your focus towards all the possibility and the opportunities that exist for you right now, then you open a whole new door. You'll push farther than you would've before. You'll try again after you fail. You'll let things be messy and just learn through the process because you're not trying to put on a show of perfection. Belief in yourself alone will change every outcome in your business.

You can find evidence in the world of bakers who thrive and bakers who are fighting to survive in business. Both sides of the coin exist. Surround yourself with the inspirational stories. Focus your lens on the amazing things bakers are doing and realize that there's nothing different between them and you. There's no secret that they have that you don't. They all started exactly where you are now!

Practice noticing your thoughts, and redirecting them when they lean south. Do things that make you feel good everyday, like taking a shower to start the day, dancing to your favorite music in the kitchen, remembering to feed yourself when you're working.

The better you feel, the better you think, the better you'll do, in business and in life.

YOUR BUSINESS PLAN

Creating a simple business plan for your bakery gives you direction and momentum. Business is frustrating when you're just throwing buttercream at the wall and hoping something sticks. Having a plan helps you know what your real goals are as a baker in business, defines you policies and procedures, helps you zero in on who you serve and how, and allows you to filter out the business activities that don't align with your plan.

YOUR PRODUCT

Of course, your actual product does play a crucial role in your business! It's important not only to fine-tune the taste, texture, and appearance of your baked goods, but also to fine-tune your production processes. Eliminating bottlenecks in production, getting in the rhythm of an efficient production schedule, and naturally improving your ability to bake and decorate will allow your business to operate smoothly, and will minimize the mental stress on you as the owner.

YOUR PRICING

A price is basically a contract between you and your customer. The "right" price for every baker is different, because it depends on your costs, your time, your expertise, and your market. The right price for your products will cover all your production costs, compensate you well for your labor, and gain a profit to reinvest in your business so growth can continue. There are customers willing to pay at every price point if you can effectively communicate the value of your product.

YOUR MARKETING STRATEGY

No one can buy from you if they don't know you exist! Marketing your businesses is all about reaching the right customers in the right way, and that is what we'll be diving into in detail throughout the rest of this book!

YOUR CUSTOMER SERVICE

Business transactions are all about trust. The customer is trusting you with their money in hopes that you'll be able to follow through on their order. When you have excellent customer service and communication skills as a business owner, that trust is formed easily and readily. Creating a profession and exceptional experience for clients throughout the entire ordering process is what will set your business apart.

YOUR FINANCE MANAGEMENT

Once a customer pays you and that revenue lands in your checking account, then what? It's critical to learn good habits with your money and get a handle on how to manage the cash flow in your business. Mastering your financial management enables you to take control of your business and empowers incredible growth.

Everything you're trying to achieve with your baking business and every challenge you feel like you're facing boils down to these six key ingredients. You can solve any business problem by turning to this recipe to see what needs adjusting.

My own baking business has given me so much. I'm a mom with two kids who was faced with a decision: Either make this baking business thing work, or go get a job to help support our family. Blessed with encouragement from my family, I chose to go the business route.

My baking business has given me so much freedom. I get to control my own schedule. I have the ability to work from home and be with my kids. I have control over my own income and finances. I feel so blessed to have come this far with my business and grateful for what it's done for my family.

And I also know it wasn't just luck.

Now I want to be the resource for you that I wish I'd had when I started out. I want to awaken you to the real possibility of success in your baking business and give you the encouragement, tools and resources to actually do it.

You deserve to take control of your life through work that you love and are paid well to do!

If you use your creativity, passion, and purpose to follow this six ingredient recipe you will find success in business.

Introduction:

Where Are All the Customers?

People have a need for baked goods. Maybe that sounds like a bit of an overstatement, but it's true. People have a *need* for those deliciously soft and decadent cupcakes that you make, or the beautiful, delicate cake designs that you craft. It is an actual bona fide need. Because the desire for baked goods goes deeper than just the utilitarian function of consumption.

A custom sweet treat is about more than just eating for the caloric energy to keep your body running. Baked goods are an *experience*. They mark memories and moments in life that went beyond just the ordinary day. They bring people together and give them a reason to gather and celebrate. A perfectly scrumptious slice of cake satisfies not just the cravings of your sweet tooth, but the emotional craving we all have inside for something more than just the everyday routine.

And in that sense, people very much have a need for baked goods that can serve up something special to help remind them that life is sweet. There are hundreds of people out there who need what you have.

But if this is true, then you're probably asking the question:

"So where are all these customers then? If people need what I have, and you say they're out there, then where is the line out the door and around the corner of people filling up my books and placing orders? How come I don't see that?"

I can answer this question with a story. A personal experience I had as a customer. My little brother was living a few states away in Michigan and was experiencing a low time in his life. He was serving as a missionary during the Covid-19 pandemic, and it was rough work trying to serve and connect with people when you couldn't be face-to-face. To top it all off, it was the coldest part of winter in Michigan, and the frigid weather wasn't doing much to help an already feeble positive attitude. With Valentine's Day coming up, I thought it would be a fun surprise to find a custom cookie baker in his area and order some fun, tasty cookies to be sent to him and his friends there.

There I was, an eager customer ready to drop $60 for a cookie order. And do you know what happened?

I didn't place the order.

Why? Because I could not find one single cookie baker in the entire state of Michigan.

And I found myself asking the opposite question: "Where are all the bakers???"

The number one reason you're not getting orders is people just don't know you exist. That's it! That's the reason!

As a home baker in business, one of the biggest qualms you face is how to get more customers. How to keep people coming through the door. Because if you're consistently gaining customers and filling your booking schedule, that is the number one sign that you're on the right path.

And this my friend, is where marketing comes into play.

Chapter 1

Welcome to Marketing 101!

"Waiting for perfect is never as smart as making progress."
Seth Godin

The word "marketing" can sound like a fancy, complicated, expensive endeavor that's only an option on the table for bigger businesses with bigger budgets. But marketing at its core is just communication. And good marketing is communicating in a way that's distinctly relatable to people. So literally anytime you tell someone about your baking business, congratulations! You're marketing!

It's easy to feel repelled by the idea of marketing for fear of being "salesy". The last thing you want to do is feel like you're being a sleazy salesman and trying to convince people to pay you for something they don't actually need. Maybe you've avoided marketing for this very reason– selling feels uncomfortable. It's way too personal.

Well, here's the wake up call: Your business isn't about you.

What you do and what you make isn't actually about you. When you put yourself out there selling your baked goods, you're actually helping someone else write their own story. When someone buys something from you, it's actually not a story about you at all. It's a story about them, their journey, and how your product becomes a part of it and helps them along to win the day. This is the true reality of what is happening in your business!

Think back to the experience I shared about trying to buy cookies for my little brother. I was trying to write this story about how he wasn't on his own and how his big sister was thinking of him and hoping he could have one bright spot in the day. Wasn't it a bummer that no one was there to help me create this story?

Going into business is about you raising your hand to say that you're available to help people write their stories. You serve them. You provide something of value to them. People need what you make, and you're there to provide solutions. When you hold back because your own ego is too afraid of the possibility of rejection and failure, and too afraid to be seen as "salesy", you actually take away someone else's choice. They would choose to order custom baked goods, just like me with my brother's cookies, but without you that choice isn't available to them.

The Spotlight Effect

Have you ever hesitated to post on social media about your

business because you were afraid that people were sick of hearing about it? If you're posting about everyday, isn't that going to bother people? You may be feeling that way, but I can guarantee you that no one else does. What's happening is a little something called the Spotlight Effect.

You are so up close to your business; it's actively running through your thoughts and you're constantly making plans around it. It's very personal to you and you're tied to it in a very emotional way. Every time you mention it or post about it, you feel like you just stepped into the spotlight. It feels like everyone now knows everything that you're doing. Everyone just saw that post and made a judgment about it, and now everyone is watching.

I remember feeling way too when I first started an Instagram for my cake business. I constantly felt that I was sharing way too much. But time and time again experience gave me the evidence to realize that wasn't the case. You would not believe how many times I would spend a month talking about my upcoming cake class on Instagram, and a friend would later say to me, "Oh! I had no idea that you just hosted a cake class! I totally would've come!"

Even now as I've become a business coach and started marketing my services as The Out-of-Home Baker, I still get friends, family, and neighbors telling me, "Oh! I had NO idea that you did that too!"

After two years of what felt to me like talking about it non-stop, 332 social media posts about it, and an audience of 50k followers, it's so intriguing to realize that my business is still completely invisible to some people.

Not everything you post shows up on someone's feed. What you do to market your business is never seen by everyone. And when they do see what you're doing, they don't always remember it. It doesn't stay fresh in their minds like it does in yours.

So what's the big takeaway here? You literally cannot talk about your business enough!

In marketing it has been statistically proven that it takes your customers an average of seven times seeing your product or brand before they will remember it and before they will be ready to purchase from you. You can see how one little handout or post isn't going to hit that mark. You've got to keep people seeing your business and interacting with it if you want it to make a real difference.

Does this mean you keep making and sending sales pitches out into the void until you've hit the magic number of seven? Not quite. Marketing isn't just about the act of advertising– *It's about the message*. It's about the people, and why what you do matters to them. And that's what this book is all about. It's not just about the mechanics of how to build a website or how to use hashtags. It's about understanding the emotional and psychological programs that are driving the market. Peoples' brains are programmed to filter out any information that doesn't pertain to its survival, so you have to make your marketing efforts relate back to your customer or they will get tuned out. Remember, your business isn't actually about you; It's about them.

Experiment and Get Messy!

Can you think back to your grade school days when you were required to make a science fair project? Those old familiar tri-fold poster boards plastered in paragraphs about hypothesis, experiment results and data? You're going to take that good old scientific method- observing a problem, creating a hypothesis, testing it out, gathering and analyzing the data- and you're going to put it to ultimate use in your business.

If you think about it, starting and growing a business is actually all about the exact same concepts you find in the scientific method: problems, hypotheses, testing, learning from the results, and then fine-tuning your experiment to see if you can get a different outcome the next time.

THE SCIENTIFIC PROCESS - BAKER STYLE

Hypothesis	Research	Experiment	Results	Tweak & Repeat
If I sell Christmas cookie dough, people will buy it and I will make a profit	How to make and package dough. Figure out who I'm trying to sell to.	Launch and complete cookie dough sale.	Had 10 orders. Was a lot of work for little return. Not as many customers as hoped for.	People want baked cookies, not dough. Next sale will try selling baked cookies prepped for decorating.

In business, this process is how you really understand what your target customers need and begin to really nail down your offer. If you want to succeed in your baking business, you have to be willing to take chances, make mistakes, and get messy! (Yes, I just Mrs. Frizzle-ed you. If you know, you know). Only by being willing to try and give it a go will you learn what works and what doesn't.

When it comes to marketing your business, treat it like a big experiment. When the results don't turn out the way you were hoping doesn't mean that it's time to quit. It means that it's time to analyze and ask yourself, "Why didn't that work? How could I change what I do next time to achieve a better result?"

You can put this principle into effect no matter what type of marketing method you're employing for your baking business. For example, I recently used an experiment to test what type of Facebook ad would work best to advertise a baking event I was hosting. Before I committed my event marketing budget to this paid ad I wanted to see what type of audience would respond the best to it. So I made two test ads and ran them at the same time for the same three days and paid just $7 each for them. The goal with the ads at this point wasn't to actually get customers yet; I just wanted to see which ad would perform the best. I wanted to test which one would get the most reach and the most link clicks.

It was very clear at the end of this little test that one of my ads was much more effective. That ad had reached thousands more, and had a much higher rate of engagement than the other. I was then able to confidently allocate more of my marketing budget towards that particular ad, and effectively helped drive traffic to my event registration page.

Be Your Own Best Cheerleader

I've worked with a lot of bakers over the past few years. I've had group calls, one-on-one sessions, and DM conversations with probably thousands of bakers at this point. All of them are trying to achieve the same goal that you are: Get your baking business up and running smoothly towards success and profit.

Bakers come to me with different challenges and concerns; everything from "I'm not getting any customers" to "I have no idea how to price things" to "I haven't found my style yet."

I faced the exact same questions and concerns when I was starting my own baking business. As I've talked with these bakers however, and analyzed their situations, and reflected on my own journey, it's become very clear to me what is at the core of all these challenges: Fear.

It's really not about a lack of knowledge or a lack of resources. We live in a day when almost everything we could possibly need to learn is at our fingertips, and a lot of it is freely available. You need to learn how to crumb coat a buttercream cake? Cool, here are 1,000 YouTube videos that will walk you through it. You don't know how to make Instagram Reels to advertise your business? No problem, there are a million Instagram coaches out there literally showing you how.

This begs the question: If the solution for everything you need to learn is right here available in front of you, why don't you learn it?

The answer is fear. We're afraid to invest time, energy, and money into learning and practicing if we're not sure it's going to pay off.

We're afraid to look like an idiot if we fail. We're afraid of what people will think. We're afraid of the risk. We're afraid of the uncertainty.

But one thing is certain: Everything you need to learn is on the other side of getting started. For this reason, I actually don't believe in failure. Every time you try, you gain a bit of knowledge. You improve your skills a little bit. You learn something you didn't know before, and that carries you on to the next try. With each try you get closer to your goal, and you start closer to it than you did before.

Trying will always get you closer to your goal than not trying.

Your ability to succeed with your baking business has everything to do with your mindset. If you let fear hold you back, you will not take the right steps forward to see success in your business. You won't put in the required energy to propel it forward.

Our brains run like algorithms, the same way your social media feed does. The more that you like, view, or engage with specific types of content, the more that the Instagram algorithm will put similar types of content into your feed. The same phenomenon can be observed outside of the digital world too. Have you ever bought a car that was a model or brand you hadn't really noticed before, but the day after you purchase it suddenly you see that type of car everywhere you go? That's because now it's at the forefront of your thoughts. Now your attention has been drawn to it.

Directing your mindset and thoughts about your business

operates the same way. If you've already decided in your head that business is going to be hard, that customers won't want to pay, and that it's going to be nearly impossible to succeed, then guess what? That's exactly what you're going to see.

Your brain will automatically search for and feed to you the evidence to support these beliefs. From our beliefs spring our feelings, thoughts, and actions. Therefore, if your beliefs center on limitations and difficulties, the reality you create in your business through your actions will reflect exactly that.

The opposite is true as well– if you focus on possibility, potential, and positive belief, that is the kind of energy that you will bring to your actions in business and the outcomes will reflect and align with those beliefs. Feed the algorithm of your brain a healthy diet of possibility and it will gladly search for evidence and data to support that!

The biggest driving force to get this business thing to work is getting yourself to believe it will. You have to become your own best cheerleader! I love to surround myself with inspirational stories of entrepreneurs– some bakers and some not– to draw on their positive energy. Listening to success stories of other entrepreneurs who started in a similar place as you is a powerful battery to fuel your motivation. At this point, I've read and heard too many of these incredible success stories to believe that a lack of resources can hold you back. Too many of the world's greatest entrepreneurs started with nothing– no expertise, no funding, no connections. And yet they're building empires that serve the world. It all starts with your ability to believe in it.

Chapter 2

Crafting Your Message

"Good marketing makes the company look smart. Great marketing makes the customer feel smart."

Joe Chernov

Effective marketing starts long before you write an ad, a post, or an email. We'll dive into more detail about the actual mechanics of marketing in a later chapter, but just know that the mechanics deal with *how* you deliver your marketing message to your customers. So it only makes sense that we need to figure out what the message is first!

When I say "message", I don't mean the caption or the actual copy that you might write. The message of your business is the higher-level bird's eye view of *why* your business is of value to the customer.

What is the mission?
What are the values?
What's the bigger vision behind serving the customer?

The message of your business & brand consists of all of this wrapped together, and then it drives everything about how you communicate to your customers regarding your products and your services.

It's easy to be wrapped up in your own founder story as the business owner. It's easy to pick brand colors that *you* like, create a logo that fits *your* aesthetic, and constantly think about what *you're* trying to get out of this business venture. We get tunnel vision. But business is a two way street. Human brains filter out anything that isn't necessary to their needs.

Let's say a customer scrolls across a post from you on social media. They may think what you're doing is great, maybe even drop you a like. But if they can't connect your content and your message in a relevant way to their own life, their brain will not store and process the information to access later. It will be sifted out to make room for information pertinent to that person's needs.

It's not to say that your story as a founder isn't important; It's a huge deal! You should share it and make it known. People like to do business with people. Showing your face and sharing your story helps build that trusting relationship with customers. But your founder story is different from the forefront story of your brand that leads in your marketing efforts.

To really craft a message and a brand that means something to your customers, you have to build it around *them*.

Who Are You Selling To?

The perfect way to begin crafting your message is to start by actually defining who your target customer is. In writing, this is called Defining Your Audience. You can't craft the perfect message to someone if you don't know who they are! Defining your target customer takes research, observation, and conversation.

First, look around at the market. What do you notice about the typical customer buying custom baked goods? What types of people have purchased from bakers or bakeries similar to you? Look for patterns in demographics and psychographics.

Let's stop and define those terms:

Demographics: Statistical data about a person or group of people that is measurable and definable. Age range, income level, and city of residence are all examples of demographic data.

Example: Females age 24-35, living in Utah Valley area, average household income between $80k to $100k, married, 2-3 kids

Psychographics: Internal factors about a person or group of people regarding their attitudes, beliefs, personality, and lifestyle. Psychographic data is dependent on subjective observation. Being extroverted vs. introverted, religious or non-religious, fashion savvy or thrifty are all examples of psychographic data.

Example: Style conscious, enjoys planning parties & events, hosts "Bachelor" night every Tuesday with girl friends, has Vasa gym membership, loves shopping at Target

The reality of being humans living on planet Earth is that making connections and finding patterns in people helps us to understand and interpret our world. Studying demographics and psychographics is not about excluding people who don't fit your mold. As business owners, understanding these factors actually allows us to better serve the customers in our little niche of the business world.

Second, if you have past customers, look at them. Who has been buying from you, and why? What's been important to them as they've gone through the order process with you? What types of events are they purchasing baked goods for?

Third, take a look at similar businesses in your industry. Party planners, photographers, venues, balloon arch artists, etc. Who are their customers? What types of people are they serving in what ways?

Pause a moment to truly think about these questions and brainstorm:

Who is your target customer?

You may not have a clear picture of who they are right now. Your understanding of your target customer will continue to develop over time. That's okay! We're always in a learning stage as business owners. We're always tweaking and pivoting, growing and fine-tuning. Never let what you don't know get in the way of getting started. The pieces of information that you're missing lay ahead of you on the journey and the only way to reach them and attain them is to just get moving.

Defining your target customer may be one of these moments. Just do your best to make the observations that you can now, and then be consciously learning about your customers as you move forward.

You may find down the road that your target customer changes, or that they're actually not who you thought they were and you've been focusing on the wrong customer group. This happened to me when I started shifting into a more creative and whimsical aesthetic for my wedding cakes. They came at a higher price, and almost intuitively I was able to perceive that my target market had shifted to a completely different group of people. It had changed from younger couples with low budgets and short engagements to older couples with long engagements, which tends to correlate with a higher budget and higher preference for style. Understanding this shift in my target customer changed everything about where and how I was marketing my cake business. Knowing who your target customer is drives it all.

The Customer's Journey

One of my all time favorite business coaches is Donald Miller, author of Business Made Simple and host of the accompanying podcast Business Made Simple. Donald Miller is another example of how you can build incredible things from nothing, himself coming from a low income family, low academic performance in school, and no prestigious college degree to his name. He is a writer and his incredible ability to connect with people through story is the bread and butter of what good marketing is all about.

He compares business and branding to a commonly used model for plot and character development called the Hero's Journey.

A story built using the Hero's Journey arc begins by presenting an average person who is just going along in normal life when they're suddenly confronted with a problem or great challenge. They begin a journey-- whether physical, emotional, or oftentimes both-- to overcome that challenge.

The catalyst to their success then comes along in the form of a guide. Someone who knows the terrain, the secrets, the strategy. With the help of this guide, the hero is able to win the day, overcome the challenge, and complete their journey.

The Hero's Journey arc is used constantly in storytelling, because it's so easy for audiences to resonate with. We can see ourselves in the same shoes as the heroes. We relate to their struggles. We love to see them overcome the challenge and come out on top! We feel like it's a story about ourselves winning the day.

You see examples of the Hero's Journey played out in many well-known books and movies: Harry Potter. Lord of the Rings. Star Wars. Heck, you can even find it in The Great British Bake Off! You watch ordinary people do extraordinary things, and there's always a guide that comes along to help them.

Using the Hero's Journey as a storytelling plot device is a brilliant way of marketing your message!

Remember how humans naturally tune out anything that is irrelevant to themselves? Storytelling can be a tool to flip the script and point the spotlight on the customer, their journey, and their challenges. It transforms your business into something that is actually relevant to them. When you use storytelling in your messaging, you position your customer as the hero. You zoom in on the specific problem that they are facing. And then you position yourself as the guide who comes along with the solution to help the hero win the day.

That's honestly the entire reason anyone buys anything—they want to win the day and be the hero of their own story. They want to create the experience, the feelings, and the reality that they've been dreaming of.

Dr. J.J. Peterson, a partner and guest on Donald Miller's Business Made Simple platform, often teaches about what really drives buying decisions and it has forever changed the way I look at commerce.

He explains that there are three levels of need driving a customer's purchases: Physical, emotional, and psychological.

> **Physical.** This is the immediate surface level need that brings us to the marketplace as customers. I accidentally put butter on my bread before putting it in the toaster, the toaster caught fire, and now I need a new toaster. That's an obvious physical need.

Emotional. While a physical need is what often drives us to look for a product or service, we actually make our buying decisions based on *emotional needs.* This boils down to how we hope to feel from a product or service. Physical need: I need a way to toast my bread. Emotional need: I want to feel in style, cohesive, and tasteful in my home so I'll buy the toaster that comes in the specific color I want.

Or maybe it's a different emotional need: I want to feel safe and in control of my finances so I'll buy a used toaster from Facebook Marketplace.

Or it could even be: I like to feel like a trendsetter so I'm going to skip the toaster altogether and buy the newest, latest gadget available to toast bread.

Can you see how the emotional need that is motivating a customer's purchasing choices can be a powerful driving force for the products you offer in your business and how you present them? While a physical need is what makes a customer search for products and services, it's ultimately the underlying emotional need that is the deciding factor in who, when, and where they buy from.

Take a moment to think about your own latest purchase. Can you identify the deeper emotional need that influenced when, where, and from whom you made the purchase?

Psychological. Dr. J.J. takes it even further and identifies a third level of need influencing customers, which is Psychological. This is the underlying belief that drives the emotional need. If I buy a toaster that is a lovely shade of mint green because matching my other kitchen decor is highly important to me, the deeper underlying psychological message might be "I deserve to feel good in my own space." The psychological need of a customer is something that they would rally around and cheer for. Framing it as an "I deserve..." statement is often helpful to identify it. "I deserve to have affordable appliances." "I deserve to experience the newest luxuries."

When you take all these points into account– the journey of your customer (the hero), and the physical, emotional, and psychological needs they have– and use story to present them in your messaging, the increased effectiveness in connecting with that customer is astounding.

How to Switch the Script

Let's put these principles into action and practice writing marketing copy that speaks to the true needs and problems of a customer.

Say you're selling homemade cinnamon rolls. You hop onto Instagram, select a picture of your product, and then you write a caption something like this:

"I'm selling cinnamon rolls this week! I've been working on my recipe and I've finally perfected it- I can't wait to share it with you! If you'd like to order some, they're $20/dz and you can just message me with your order. Pick up will be on Friday night."

It's not bad; and if that's the type of captions you've been writing, it's a fantastic start!! You hit all the information and you put yourself out there! I just want to recognize and celebrate that with you, because taking steps to market your business can be so intimidating, and the fact that you've been doing this is a beautiful, courageous feat. Many don't even make it that far.

So now, let's use storytelling to elevate the effectiveness of your post and your marketing. Right now, the story being told is all focused on you. It's about what you're doing, what you've achieved, and what you want.

But what's your customer's story? Maybe you know the people who tend to buy your cinnamon rolls are busy moms in your neighborhood with busy kids, and your cinnamon rolls make a delicious, easy weekend breakfast for families. There's a story starting to form here: A mom who runs around all week trying her best to take good care of her kids and she needs a well-deserved break. She needs a reward. She needs ease. And she needs her kids to be fed and happy.

So let's take this information and take another crack at this caption:

> "*I see you, Momma:*
>
> *You drove to the school 25 times this week to pick up kids.*
> *You cleaned the living room 15 times (only to have it messed up again).*
> *You worked hard all week to keep those kiddos clean and fed and happy.*
>
> *I'm officially declaring that Saturday is your day for just a little break and a little reward for you (okay, and the kids) for surviving another week! Cinnamon roll pick up is this Friday night, so you can have a tasty, fresh, homemade Saturday breakfast ready to go. No dishes or clean up required.*
>
> *Pans are $20/dz. Use my order form to order. Pick up is Friday night, but girl, if you need delivery I've got you!*"

Holy cow! My mouth is watering and I'm going to have to go find me a cinnamon roll baker because that caption meant something to me! That's the power of storytelling. That's the power of understanding your target customer.

Chapter 3

Building Your Brand Identity

"A brand is no longer what we tell the consumer it is- it's what consumers tell each other it is."

Scott Cook

••

Brand is a word that has become such a buzz in our modern society. It gets tossed here and there all over the place. Building a *brand*. *Brand* deals. Whether things are *on-brand* or *off-brand*.

But what is a *brand,* actually?

Our initial understanding of a brand typically doesn't go beyond a logo. If someone asks you what brand of cereal you like the best, chances are it's the logo that pops right into your head. Logos are fantastic visual symbols of a brand, but they are not the entirety of the brand itself. It's like the chicken vs. the egg conundrum. Which came first?

In the case of a brand, it's the message. The logo, the colors, the fonts, and the voice then come second to support and communicate that message in the most effective way possible.

Branding goes back to emotion. It's not just visual. It's everything that people feel and associate by interacting with your products and services. It's the tone of voice that speaks in your messaging. It's the connections they draw from your business to their reality. And all of that goes back to your messaging, your target customer, and the story of that customer's journey. Your brand is the vehicle to communicate all of that in a consistent and cohesive manner.

Last year, I sold a wedding cake for just over $1600 US dollars. It is to date the most expensive cake order I have ever made. Which is exciting; every time I push the boundary of what I think I can charge and sell a cake for a higher price than I have before, it continues to help break down my own persisting mental barriers around price and money in business. After all, if someone paid me $1600 once for a wedding cake, why can't it happen again and again all the time? And then why can't it be $2000? Many of the limits and roadblocks we perceive often exist only in our own minds. Your own mind represents the greatest barrier to your success in business.

I sold and was paid in full for this high-ticket wedding cake. Bakers often ask me, "How do you get those higher paying clients?! I can barely get someone to pay me $100!"

The answer is branding.

A customer's brain is always subconsciously analyzing everything. How we show up in front of potential customers sends a message, and they're interpreting that message and drawing conclusions about it, whether they even realize it or not.

Have you ever felt like there's a stigma around home-based bakers? That people imply that if you're baking at home, you shouldn't have to be paid as much? We get a bad rap, and it's frustrating. But the tough-love truth is that we don't do enough to negate those subconscious, low valuations customers give to our products and services.

At the beginning of this book, I introduced you to the recipe for success in business. There were six key ingredients in that recipe:

A plan, your product, your price, your marketing, your customer service, and your financial management.

It takes a focus on all six of those ingredients in order to hit your highest potential and success as a baker in business. We easily get caught up in the product: How can I improve my recipes, my decorating, my buttercream? What other things can I add to my menu? But if you want to book more clients and especially more high end clients, then you have to think just beyond the product itself.

Let's talk about Disneyland. Imagine for a moment if you took all the physical rides themselves out of the park and set them up again in an empty lot somewhere. Would you still pay the current rate for Disneyland admission to ride them in that empty lot? That's a big nope.

Because it's almost not even about the rides themselves. What park goers are interested in is the entire experience, and the rides are just a part of that.

Your job as the baking business owner is to create a Disneyland level experience for your customers. From the moment they roll up, there's a feeling communicated that lets them know they came to the right place. They feel welcome, validated, and seen. There's a visual consistency that builds trust because it signals to them that this isn't your first rodeo. You've put thought and effort into this. You take this seriously. That, my friend, is what allows someone to pay top dollar for your work, just like the millions each year who pay top dollar to go to Disneyland.

Define the Vibe of Your Brand Identity

Before you dive into choosing colors and fonts, you'll want to define the overall vibe of your brand that you're aiming to communicate. Now it's time to pull out your notes from the previous chapter about your message and target customer, because that is where you'll find the feelings, emotions, and imagery to fuel the creation of your brand identity.

Take a moment to brainstorm a list of words and feelings that describe the message you want to communicate.

Here's an example of a word brainstorm for a Cake Pop Business:

-Fun	*-Smiling*	*-Colorful*
-Mini	*-Over-the-top*	*-Personal*
-Party	*-Kids*	*-Sprinkles*
-Celebration	*-Detailed*	*-Excitement*

From the words you wrote on your list, can you start to catch the vision for your brand identity? As you create each characteristic element for your brand, everything should tie back to the words and feelings from the list you just made.

Creating a Style Guide

The purpose of a style guide is to help streamline the creation of all your marketing visuals and graphics so they all fit together cohesively and maintain a consistent look across all of your marketing.

One of my favorite tools for creating *everything*, including style guides, graphics, and visuals, is an app called Canva. You can play around with color palettes, stock images and graphics, font pairings, and access easy-to-use templates for creating media for any platform. This is a completely unsponsored and shameless plug for the app- I love it! And I will continue to evangelize it as a priority app to have as a business owner.

Color: First, define the color palette of your brand. Pick a main color, plus two supporting colors that represent. These colors should be cohesive together and should complement each other instead of competing.

Color plays a fascinating role in the marketing world and its influence is not to be taken for granted. Without even realizing it, we assign specific meanings and feelings to colors, and they can stimulate specific associations in our minds.

For instance, red tends to trigger hunger. Fast food restaurants have obviously clued in on this detail. How many fast food establishments can you think of who's main brand color is red? Chick-fil-A, Wendy's, Panda Express, Arby's, McDonald's. I could go on and on.

To help you pick appropriate colors to represent the message you want to communicate with your brand, here's a list of colors and typical meanings and associations that we give to them:

Warm Colors

Magenta, Red, Orange, Yellow

These colors tend to increase psychological stimulation, and are commonly used in the fast food industry, retail, healthcare advocacy, and the transportation industry.

Red: Symbolizes energy, passion, love, sacrifice, danger, heat, anger, activity

Orange: Optimism, positivity, creativity, excitement, high-energy

Yellow: Youthful, fresh, cheerful, optimism, hope, curiosity, warning, caution

Cool Colors

Green, Blue, Indigo, Purple

These colors bring an overall feeling of tranquility and trust. Commonly used in financial institutions, technology, hospitality, healthcare, and law enforcement.

Green: Fresh, earth, rebirth, new growth, envy, jealousy, lack of experience

Blue: Sky, sea, freedom, intuition, imagination, inspiration, cold, calm, wisdom, stability, trust

Purple: Creativity, royalty, spirituality, wealth, power, grandeur, mystery, magic

Neutrals

Black, Grey, White, Brown, Tan

These colors bring a sense of luxury, and coordinate well with many other colors, making them versatile players in branding. Commonly used in the luxury car industry, designer clothing, and upscale businesses.

Black: Mystery, power, sophistication, elegance, urgency, evil, death

White: Purity, cleanliness, safety, space, neutrality, peace, truth

Gray: Control, compromise, balance, depression, uncertainty

Brown/tan: Strength, reliability, earth, resilience, dependability, warmth

Typography: Next, we'll look at fonts. A simple format is to select a main font for titles, a supporting font for subtitles, and a good, nice font for body text. Again, it's subtle, but font styles and typography can do a lot to aid in the visual communication of the message your brand stands for.

Now, no matter what lettering style you decide to choose, one thing always takes precedence: **readability**. I don't care how pretty your curly-cue letters are if I have to squint to decipher them!

You need to define not only the fonts, but also define the style specifications:

Is it bolded?
Is it italicized?
What is the letter spacing?
What is the set font size for titles, subtitles, and body text?

Defining all of this not only provides consistency in your branding that allows customers to recognize your content faster, but it also helps you in creating content because you won't need to sift through fonts and mess around with style specifications every time you want to make an ad. You'll already have guiding points to reference as you create content for your brand.

As an un-written rule from the world of graphic design, just consider the fonts Papyrus and Comic Sans to be off limits. Don't ask me what it is exactly, but something about those two fonts just screams middle-grade kid messing around in PowerPoint for the first time.

HEADINGS/TITLES
Font: Glacial Indifference, Size: 32, Letter Spacing: 320

SUBTITLES
Font: Glacial Indifference, Size: 18, Letter Spacing: 320

SUBHEADINGS
Font: Glacial Indifference, Bold, Size: 14, Letter Spacing: 320

Body text
Font: Times Neue Roman, Size: 12, Letter Spacing: 34

Creating a Logo

Time to cash in on some of my personal connections to the professional world of graphic design, namely my husband Nate. He graduated from the BYU Illustration program with his bachelor's degree, and has spent the past several years working as a designer for many different companies. He also teaches a university level class on Intro to Graphic Design. One of the projects his students have to complete is logo design, and I often hear him recording feedback for students on their work. At some point I realized this was really useful stuff for my own business, so I pulled out my mental clipboard and started taking notes, which I now bring to you.

The first thing to address about logos right off the bat: there is a difference between an illustration and a logo, and they do not serve the same purpose.

A logo is a very simple, recognizable, graphic design that represents your business, your purpose, and your products. Think of the iconic "swoosh" used as the logo for Nike.

An illustration is a colorful, more complex graphic that can be used as a marketing tool, but it is not the flagship image that should represent your business. Think of an illustrated mascot design, or the caricature avatar illustrations that you see crop up on social media. They're fun to have and can help in the marketing of your brand, but shouldn't stand in for a proper logo.

Logo:
A simple graphic to represent your business

Illustration:
A more complex artwork that can be used for marketing

The main difference that sets a logo apart from an illustration is versatility. A logo needs to be usable in many different forms and sizes. You might blow it up big for an event banner, or you may need to shrink it down to fit on your business cards. A good logo will maintain its integrity as a design in any size, across all printing and digital formats. An illustration with multiple colors, small intricate details, and gradients doesn't lend well to consistency across formats.

A logo is meant to be memorable in the mind of a customer. The simpler the design, the easier to remember. An illustration is too busy for a customer's mind to process quickly. It doesn't always translate well to bigger and smaller sizes, and if you have to print it in a black and white, you lose a lot of the impact of the original color design.

To increase versatility, a good logo should:

-Consist of two-three colors max. This allows for simplicity and versatility in printing formats.

-Avoid gradients in the colors. These do not translate well across all printed mediums and sizes.

-Still be visually comprehensive whether printed small or large.

-Have a strong silhouette. This increases the clarity and readability of a design. If you're logo is easily recognizable when it's a black and white silhouette, then you know you have a strong image. Think of Mickey Mouse- you will always recognize his image, even when it's just a black silhouette outline.

The purpose of your logo is to help a customer understand and remember who you are as a business, what you sell, and get a clue as to what your purpose is.

The Impact of a Logo

Just a 30 minute drive from me lives one of my best friends Sheree. She also owns and runs a baking business from home called Wild Flower Cakes. But that wasn't the first name of her business. I'll never forget watching her go through a re-branding phase with her cake business and the secondhand lessons I was able to learn from it. Originally her cake business was called Cakes That Are Baked, which was a playful, fun name that well-represented her brand for years. But she started looking to break into the wedding cake industry more. She had realized that her passion lay in designing beautiful, creative wedding cakes more than it did with the character and sculpted cakes.

But she was stuck trying to make that transition.

A friend of hers mentioned that he worked in marketing and branding, and offered to take a look at her website and portfolio and give her some pointers. He was very blunt when he pulled up her site for the first time.

The first thing he said to her was: "If you want to do wedding cake orders, then why is your logo a cupcake?"

The question was so obvious and basic, but it floored her. Her succulent cupcake logo had been around since the beginning of her business, back when she did a lot of piped buttercream flowers and succulents. It was where her business story had started. But he was right! It didn't make any sense to a wedding client to order a wedding cake from a business with a succulent cupcake as its flagship image.

1ST LOGO　　　　**2ND LOGO**　　　　**3RD LOGO**

As I've watched my friend Sheree adjust and tweak her branding, the results have been incredible. She now gets ample orders that actually fit the style of cakes that she prefers to work in. A client even told her specifically that because of Sheree's business branding, specifically her business name, the client knew right away that Sheree would be the perfect fit for the client's wedding cake.

It should also be noted that just because you sell cakes or cookies doesn't necessarily mean that your logo *has* to be an image of a cake or a cookie. What do apples have to do with computers? Technically nothing. But someone says "Apple" and we all know what business and what product we're talking about. That's the power of a good logo.

As we begin to dive even more into the methods of distributing your brand and message out into the market, it's important to note that in our rapidly changing technological world, the mechanisms for marketing change constantly. New social media apps, new online sales platforms, new distribution channels are emerging all the time. Despite the changing mechanics of how you deliver your brand message, these same principles of messaging and branding will hold true and remain key.

They continue to apply across the board and across industries, whether you're marketing via TikTok, a magazine, emails, or good old-fashioned business cards.

Chapter 4

Clarity Is King

"Here's everything you need to know about creating killer content in 3 simple words: Clear. Concise. Compelling."

Demian Farnworth

●●

I was heading out on the road for a little trip and wanted to stop for food on the way out of town. I'm pretty over McDonald's and other low quality franchise restaurants, and I wanted *good* food to mark a fun day heading out on the road. But I was on a schedule, so I needed a place with a drive-through. Many of my friends had been raving about the food at this new place out by the freeway, so I decided to give it a try.

I pulled up through the driveway, but was a bit confused to see a totally blank menu screen. I waited for a voice to come over the speaker and take my order, but nobody did. So finally I spoke. "Um...hello? Is anyone there?"

"Yes! What can I get for you today?" Finally a voice crackled over the speaker.

"Well, I'm actually not sure what you have. Your menu is blank. And I'm not sure what your prices are either."

"Oh, yeah, no worries! You just tell us what you want and we'll tell you if we
have it, and then we'll tell you how much it costs"

"Uh....okay."

Would you stay in that drive thru and go back and forth with these people? Absolutely not! It's a headache and a half. I should be able to roll up and easily know what products suit my budget and placing my order should be a breeze.

This is in actuality a fictitious story. I never actually went through a blank drive thru and had this conversation, but you can clearly see the point that it illustrates.

As a business, ordering from you should be as easy as possible, or customers will abandon ship. It sounds a bit ridiculous, but people don't want to think. They don't want to put in more energy than necessary. They're busy all day long and if you're going to make them do mental gymnastics just to know what your offerings are, they're going to move along to the next, easier option.

Think about moments when you've been a customer and seen this thought process in your own experience. I can see many times when the ease of ordering played a *huge* role in who I gave my business to. When my little sister-in-law was getting married, I was helping my mother-in-law find all the vendors for the wedding; specifically, we needed to rent tables and chairs.

As we combed through the websites of different rental companies, if any of them didn't have pricing listed or information about how rentals worked, we didn't even bother. We had a lot to do! There wasn't time or energy to spare in taking time to reach out to everyone and wait to hear back.

The business who had all of the rental information clearly spelled out was the one that got our money.

Heck, I've even felt this when I've walked into a less-than-efficient Subway, and the person at the counter doesn't give me any guidance as to what information they need from me in order to take my order. If I get a blank look and have to ask, "Um...how does this work again?" It really makes me want to just turn around and find somewhere else to eat. Confused customers don't buy!

Customers looking for baked goods are no different! It's not unusual for your average client to be not only booking a cake, cookies, and desserts, but planning an entire event with their focus spread all over the place. They need ordering processes that are quick, easy, simple, and efficient.

How do you create this for your customers? The answer is Clarity.

Creating Clarity in Your Business

Clarity is a customer's ability to understand, almost instantly, what you sell, who you serve, and how to order from you.

No matter which piece of your content they come across first, whether it's your Instagram page, website, or a printed ad, clarity will allow your brand message to come across quickly in the minds of your customers.

How you show up matters, especially when it comes to booking higher ticket clients. When there is clarity and professionalism surrounding your brand, your products, and your order process, the higher prices go down easier without the nit-picky budget battles, because the client trusts you as a business.

Clarity in your branding:

We've talked a lot about branding and how it's more than visuals and graphics you use-- It's also the emotions, voice, and experiences that customers associate with your business. As you build your brand identity, keep clarity in mind. The brand won't matter much (or at least won't be as impactful to customers) if it's difficult to understand and apply to themselves.

Clarity in branding is created through simplicity, consistency, and readability. Keep things simple with your brand by focusing on the niche that you serve. When you try to be everything for everyone, you end up being of minimal importance to anyone. Your brand doesn't need to resonate with every type of customer, just the people who are your target customer.

Consistency in branding builds clarity because it allows a customer to easily tie your marketing back to your business based on visual cues, like color, font, and style.

Readability always trumps design, because the design doesn't matter much if it can't be read. If people have to squint at a squiggly font or pick out light colored letters on a light colored background, then clarity is lacking.

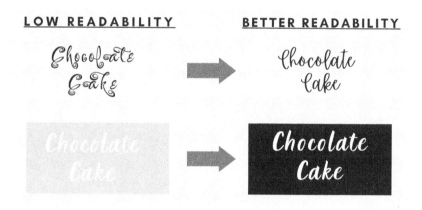

Create clarity through transparency:

You should never feel like you have to trick people into going through the order process with you before revealing hidden details such as pricing info, booking and payment policies, or contract terms and conditions. Clarity is created when you answer customer questions before they have them. This shortens the order process, and helps ensure that the people inquiring with you are serious customers. It also saves a lot of your own valuable time. As a business owner, you wear a lot of hats and you have a lot of things demanding your focus. The last thing you need to spend time on is a back-and-forth conversation with a customer who isn't a serious customer.

Controversy and differing opinions exist around whether or not you should make your pricing visible to customers before they inquire, but I myself am 100% pro-transparent pricing! For obvious reasons as a custom baker, you won't be able to transparently outline the specific price points for every possible order. Many of us don't work at flat rates because goods are made to the specifications of the customer, and each product is unique. But that doesn't mean you can't find a way to at least give the customer an idea of your price range. They need to know right off the bat if you're a good fit for their budget.

Will you lose customers over this? Yes—the ones who weren't going to order from you anyways!

What a waste of time it is to go through multiple conversations with a client to finally arrive at the topic of price, only to have the client realize your work was never within their budget to begin with.

And don't forget how many people walk away when they can't discern right away whether or not you're a good fit for them. You will always lose more customers by not posting your prices than you will by posting them.

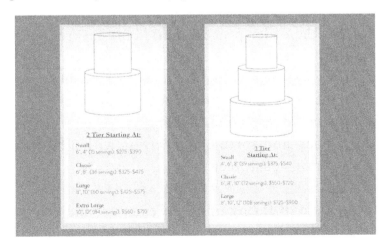

Create clarity through excellent communication:

Clear and professional communication is essential for clarity in your business. This includes your communication through the text and copy you write for ads, the messages and emails you write to customers, and even communication through the images that you use. Practicing and applying excellent communication skills will set you apart as an expert, and people will feel safe putting their orders in your hands. How you communicate all goes back to knowing that it's more than just a product that you provide for people—it's an experience.

Many misunderstandings can be prevented before they even happen when you communicate clearly with your customers. Always be straightforward in the dialogue you use to convey your payment policies, your delivery and pick-up procedures, and the order specifications.

If you're ever unsure of what a customer's expectations are, _make sure you ask_.

Don't just assume that they know the cake topper isn't included, or that you charge a late fee if they don't pick up on time. It's important to lay out those policies before the problem arises.

Clarity is also created through the way you communicate with your images. They say a picture is worth a thousand words, and they're right! The photos included in your portfolio will speak louder than any paragraph you could write. Our brains process images so much faster than words, and let's be honest, that's in part due to the fact that we will avoid actually reading words at any cost.

Having quality images to communicate about your products plays a huge role in the types of clients and types of orders that will come in. If you're trying to get wedding cakes booked but all your images are Paw Patrol birthday cakes, you're not going to attract the wedding clients that you want. It's as simple as that. Your images should be clear, high-quality depictions of what you actually sell. The first thing a customer should see when they come across your website, your Instagram page, or any other ad should be your best photo of your best work.

Back in 2019, I finally decided it was time to go full speed ahead as a legitimate cake business. After a few years of doing cakes here and there on the side, I went through all the steps to legally register and license my business, and I started to get very intentional about my marketing.

I knew that if I wanted to get real wedding clients, I was going to need some nice wedding cakes in my portfolio, which at that moment I did not have. So I got together with my sister, who happened to be a professional photographer, and and we had ourselves a fun little cake photoshoot!

I made two real cakes, one six inches in diameter and one eight inches, and then also had a few styrofoam dummy cake rounds. By mixing and matching tiers and floral arrangements, we were able to capture five different cake designs! She gave me back an entire portfolio of photos that were ready to be uploaded onto all my pages. Those high-quality images were enormously beneficial in spring-boarding myself onto the professional wedding scene.

Create the Simplest Order Process Possible

A few years ago, I hosted a live coaching session workshop where we actually played the role of a customer and placed a cookie order. It was a learning tool to help us as business owners to really understand what it feels like to be on the other side of placing a custom baked good order, and we completed our experiment in good faith and respect for the bakers we inquired with.

I was helping host a bridal shower for my little sister-in-law, so for our experiment we were looking for custom cookies that could be handed out as party favors at the end of the shower. We picked a design, set our budget, and set out to find a baker that would fit our needs.

We ended up inquiring with three different cookie bakers, and officially booked with one of them a day or two later. The process of ordering gave us some incredibly insightful observations:

First, we initially searched for a cookie baker on Google first, then through friend recommendations, and then finally through Instagram, which is where we found the three bakers that we inquired with. It was fascinating to see what channels we were naturally inclined to turn to when searching for custom baked goods.

Second, the cookie baker we ended up booking with was the one who had the clearest details about her products and order process before we even messaged her. We didn't have to ask her what the cost was, whether or not she could individually package the cookies, and if she could do the design we were looking for. All of those questions were answered clearly in the order process she had set up. Her order form had walked us through order sizing, costs of extra add-ons, and had packaging options for us to select. Her portfolio clearly demonstrated that she was capable of executing the design we wanted.

When she promptly responded that she was available for our order, it was an easy decision for us! We didn't have any other questions to ask. The other bakers who responded to us would've required further back and forth messaging because we were still unsure about their packaging and custom design options.

The easier it is to order from you, the more orders you'll get. It's a simple, yet powerful principle. Having a clear, streamlined order process will work wonders in the minds of your customers. It builds trust, clarity, and gets people in the door faster.

The Conversion Funnel

If you've ever heard the phrase "conversion funnel", this is where it comes into play.

Imagine a big funnel shape, with a wide opening at the top and a narrow opening at the bottom. The wide, top end is where potential customers first come in contact with your business. The smaller, narrow opening at the bottom represents potential customers who have converted into a sale, becoming actual customers.

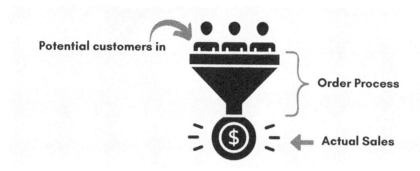

The funnel gets narrower and narrower to show how at each step in the ordering process, you'll lose people. And the more steps you have, the more and more people you'll lose before they actually purchase from you.

The conversion funnel demonstrates the need to get to the point faster with your customers. You want to collect all of their order details, give them a final price quote and request payment to book in the fewest number of steps possible.

Having an actual order form for customers to fill out is super helpful in streamlining this process. You can set up an order form in many different ways- Google forms, a website form, or a shop on Castiron, just to name a few. The point of an order form is to guide your customer in providing you with all of the essential information you need to book the order in the very first inquiry. It also helps the customer to be aware of the options that you offer.

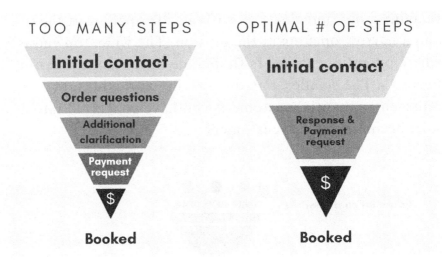

TOO MANY STEPS

Initial contact
Order questions
Additional clarification
Payment request
$

Booked

OPTIMAL # OF STEPS

Initial contact

Response & Payment request

$

Booked

Critical information to collect on an order form includes their name, contact info, event date and location, size/servings needed, flavors, and a spot to include details or submit image reference for the design. Be sure to preface the order form with a statement that it does not officially book the order.

Your order form should be easy to navigate and fill out. Keep it concise and help your customers avoid decision fatigue.

What do I mean by decision fatigue?

I once came across a baker's website who's menu had listed over 100 flavors. At first glance, this might seem like an exciting, unique value proposition to the customer. So many flavors to choose from! But let me tell you, it gets overwhelming very quickly. It creates decision fatigue for the customer, where they get frustrated with the whole process and want to be done with it.

You don't have to offer every flavor, size, and dessert under the sun. Flushing out your menu just for the sake of having a big menu doesn't actually increase the value provided to the customer. It can be incredibly beneficial to your brand to focus on just one or two product offerings at first, and really fine-tune the quality and hype around them before you continue to add to your menu and services. In entrepreneurship, they like to say "nail it, then scale it!"

Be an expert in your niche and you will amplify the quality of your product offerings, rather than just the quantity, and it will amplify the reputation of your brand.

The Power of Customer Reviews

It can scare you out of your pants to think about asking a customer for feedback. Your baking is very personal, and it can be hard to separate a critical review on your products from your own self-esteem. I know, I've been there too. Putting your creativity out there and charging for it is hard enough. To ask for feedback on it? Feels like asking too much.

However, sharing customer reviews can increase the confidence of customers in your brand and business in such a powerful way! I've done a good bit of research with my own customers over the years to find out what was critical to them in their decision to book with me. Reading customer reviews ranks number one every time.

Customer reviews build clarity around your business because it involves the experiences of real people who've purchased products from you. Nothing is more transparent than providing customers with the honest feedback of other customers.

While the emotional barriers to collecting customer reviews may feel high, it's actually pretty simple to do. A few days after a customer's order has been completed, send them a simple message thanking them for their business and asking them to leave a review. Here's a simple dialogue that you could follow when requesting reviews:

Hello [Customer's Name]!

Thank you so much again for ordering with me!

My small business thrives off of feedback and I continually strive to deliver excellent service to you. Would you be willing to leave me a quick review about your experiences ordering from my business? I would be so grateful for your thoughts!

You can use this link to leave a review: [insert form link or google review link]

Thank you again for your support of my business!

Best Regards,

[Your Name]

The goal is to keep your request short and sweet, and always add your gratitude for them as a customer.

Please don't pause your business progress until you check all of these boxes. These are things you learn and develop and improve as you take small steps forward.

If you could see the first version of my website, you might laugh out loud. It was messy. It was incoherent. It was very amateur. But I launched it anyways and it brought in orders. I continued to just build it up little by little. My website would not be what it is today if I hadn't just started anyways.

As you continue to work steadily on each of these principles and build clarity in your marketing, you will increase your customers' ability to relate with your business, understand your processes, and make ordering from you a piece of cake.

Chapter 5

Discoverability

"Your visibility is more important than your ability."
Peter Montoya

•••

I once taught a wedding cake branding workshop with my good friend Kala who runs her own designer wedding cake business, and we received a question from a baker about why she wasn't getting orders. She had worked on her brand, her messaging, and her content, but still she felt like the orders were lacking. It's a question I get all the time as a business coach.

My response to her came in the form of another simple question: "Have you explored every marketing option available to you?"

In her mind, she thought she had. Remember the Spotlight Effect? To this baker, her business was at the forefront of everything. She thinks about it 24/7 and puts a lot of her time into building it up. It was natural and understandable that to her it felt like she had exhausted every avenue possible to gain customers. Every business owner experiences this to some degree.

But then Kala followed up with a simple question that was a big eye-opener for her: "What about the venues around you? Have you met with them? Do you have their emails and phone numbers?"

She didn't! There was an entire avenue of potential for reaching new customers that she hadn't even explored yet! Kala continued to explain to her and the other bakers on the coaching call that the next step is to invite those venue owners to coffee and build a real relationship with them. Such a simple, yet game-changing concept!

The most likely culprit for why you're not getting more orders is that customers just don't know about you yet. This is where Discoverability comes into play.

There's nothing better than knowing that your marketing efforts are actually paying off. When your client tells you, "Oh I found a cake that you posted on Instagram!" or "I did a google search and you came up!" That's when you know that the channels you're using to market your business are effective.

Essentially if people are able to find your products and services when they need them, then your business is discoverable. I said it before, if customers can't find you they can't order from you. Discoverability as a business is too critical to leave it to chance. You can't just wait for the customers to roll up and order. You've got to get intentional about how you're going to lay a roadmap for customers to find you.

Imagine if you wanted to apply for a job. You have all the skills and credentials. You're well qualified with good work experience behind you to make you the perfect candidate for the position. In order to apply for the job, you would probably need to make yourself a nice little resume, right? A document that demonstrates how you're the perfect fit for the employment opportunity due to your years of experience, skills, and credentials. So you sit down and put together a fantastic resume. And then you leave it on your desk and take it to no one. How likely are you to get hired?

That's an easy one– not at all.

Even though you're the real deal and you've packaged it all up nicely, potential employers don't have a clue that you exist. So what should you do instead? Actually take that resume to someone! Submit it online! Put it out there!

This is what discoverability is all about. By reading this book and following its guidance up until this point, you've basically created your perfect resume, which is your marketing message and your branding. Now you need to "submit the resume" and actually get it in front of the right people.

In the case of the cookies I tried to order for my brother, I felt so bad for all those Michigan cookie makers (who I know exist!) because they had very low discoverability. The potential customer–me –could not find them in my time of need. Can you imagine how many other potential customers they're missing out on because of how hard they are to find?

Now that you have your message and your brand identity all polished and packaged, you're ready to dig into the actual mechanics of marketing. Let's get into the nitty gritty details of how you actually get your business out into the world and connect with the right customers.

Marketing Channels

Let's break down all the possible avenues you could use to distribute your marketing message to make your business discoverable to your customers.

There are 4 categories of marketing channels to explore: traditional print, digital, networking, and events.

1.Traditional Print

When you think of marketing through a traditional print channel, think old fashioned, hard-copy advertising. Traditional print is how people marketed their businesses long before the advent of the digital social media age. It's channels consist of printed ads in newspapers, magazines, flyers and posters, business cards that you hand out, or physical mailers that you send out to the community.

Don't overlook the power that traditional print channels still have in the marketing world. Printed marketing materials have a level of staying power that a digital ad just doesn't. This means that your ad isn't going to disappear into the void after a day, the way it would on social media. If you've got a space in a printed magazine, that marketing real estate is yours permanently. A potential customer flipping through that magazine edition will always find your ad there in that same spot where it was printed.

This also means your marketing can reach unexpected customers. There's a serendipity to real physical marketing materials in that they can end up in front of anyone.

That same serendipity can also become a disadvantage of traditional printed ads. In the digital world, you can set the specific target demographics of who you want your marketing to reach, so as to not waste your marketing resources reaching people who aren't interested in your products. The same ability to target and to get analytic feedback about your audience doesn't exist in the same way for traditional print.

Another disadvantage of printed marketing is the cost. It can quickly get expensive to invest in printed materials or ad space.

Always evaluate the target audience that the ad would be placed in front of, and the likely return on your investment. In just a moment, I'll walk you through the specific steps of how to evaluate whether a marketing opportunity is the right one for your business.

Whenever you're faced with an expensive, but shiny looking marketing opportunity that you feel like you want to jump on, take a step back and ask yourself first: What else could I do with that money that might be more effective? Chances are, you can create your own opportunity to market your business that's five times as effective at a quarter of the cost.

Occasionally, the expensive marketing investment might be the right fit. Other times, you might want to take the $1000 that you were ready to spend on a magazine ad and use it to host a few free consultations instead. The bottom line is don't get too caught up in high-cost marketing through third parties without considering your own power to market on your own.

2. Digital

The internet and social media is one of the greatest gifts to small businesses. The ability to connect instantly with potential customers online is truly incredible! Learning how to leverage the power of digital marketing will open up a world of possibilities to your business with very minimal cost on your part, other than the time investment it takes to learn the digital ropes.

There are three tiers to digital marketing:
- Utilizing free social platforms
- Building your own searchable site
- Paying for ad space, audience placement and promotion through a third party

Social Media

While an incredible tool, it's easy to you find yourself overwhelmed as a home baker trying to run social media pages for your business.

Why does it always end up taking 15 minutes to write a post?

And how many times do I have to re-film this video until I get the lip sync right?

And what if I don't have any new pictures to post? What then???

The good news: there is a strategic approach to being a small business on social media. There are a few key parts that you need to have in place in order to have success, and there are several features and metrics that you can ignore all together.

You don't have to use every feature and spend endless hours creating reels, going live and posting to your stories. You just need to focus on aspects of social media that actually help to customers find your business and to order from you.

Let's talk about a few of the aspects of social media that are not key to helping you grow your business.

1.Stop counting your followers. You are not playing a followers game. Don't get caught up chasing page growth just for the sake of page growth. Growth isn't necessarily a bad thing, but it is senseless to pour time and resources just into gaining followers. As a small business home baker, your profit comes from orders made by local customers. Instead of focusing on gaining followers, focus on reaching those local customers. Truly, your presence as a small local business actually feels more genuine and authentic to the community when you *don't* have a big following number. You can have high sales with a small following when you nurture genuine connection over reach, trends, and vanity metrics.

2. Copying a content strategy. Content Creators are those who make their money by selling some type of online product or service, or have profitable brand deals. Think of all the big, beautiful baking pages you love to follow: Cake By Courtney, Sheri Wilson, Sally's Baking Blog. Their target audiences and customers are not restricted by geographical area, because the value they create through their content is digital and accessible beyond local boundaries.

Content creators *do* focus on their following, reach and engagement metrics because those analytics correlate directly with the way they make money. They're business model is inherently very different than yours. For content creators, it's not about reaching local customers and getting orders.

Yet when you jump on social media for the first time, often you're pulled to imitate the types of content, text, and voice that content creators embody. But trying to base your social media plan off of a content creation strategy will have you spinning your wheels a million miles an hour with no profitable results.

You are an order driven baking business and you make your money based off of local orders. Your strategy on social media is going to look completely different than much of the content you come across.

3. Talking to other bakers. At first glance, this tip doesn't sound right, especially when I champion the power of connecting as a baking community. So let me explain:

As a home baker, your social media feed is probably full of content from other bakers. You see posts from bakers you follow for inspiration and you mostly interact with other bakers. So naturally, you go to write and create content, you tend to end up directing it to them. You talk to other bakers in your captions, in your stories, in your bio.

I see this especially in reels and other short videos made by bakers that essentially make fun of their customers, which is content that resonates very well with other bakers, but is not going to have a positive impact at all when a potential customer sees it.

You need to know who your actual target customer is and direct your content at them. The overall message of any piece of content you create for your business should focus on what problem your business solves for your customer, how you solve it, and how they're life will be better through your product and service.

When it comes to marketing on social media, go back to square one, which is everything we covered at the beginning of this book about your message, you target customer, your brand, and clarity. That is the key information that will guide how and where you show up on social media.

How do you know what social media platforms to even be on? By knowing who your target customer is. You don't have to run a page for your business on every social media platform to ever exist. You just need to be prevalent on the platform where your target customer demographic hangs out the most.

For my own baking business, this was Instagram. All the recently engaged bride-to-be women in my market were younger than the Facebook generation- most of them don't even have Facebook pages. So I really let my Facebook marketing sit on the back burner while I poured all of my social media efforts into my Instagram page. And it paid off!

Your first step as a business on a social media platform is to set up an all new account or page for your business that is completely separate from your personal page. Remember th importance of clarity? Customers shouldn't have to sift through photos of your dog when they're trying to see your baking portfolio (even if your dog is the cutest in the world). A separate business page allows you to show up professionally and eliminates confusion for your customers.

Your business pages and profiles should be publicly accessible and not private. It's useless for a customer if your business page is hidden from them due to privacy settings. Trust me, they will not waste time waiting for friend approval. They will move along to the next visible business.

Now, if you want potential customers to be able to find you on social media, then I've got one word for you:

Keywords.

Think about that customer searching for a product or service. What do they type in that search bar?

"Custom Cakes in Utah"
"Utah Cake Maker"
"Utah Wedding Cakes"

These are all called keywords. They relate to what you do and where you are. Brainstorm as many of these key words as you can and make a list. You use key words on your social media pages so the search robot can pull you up as a relevant result to a customer's inquiry. Without those keywords you are basically invisible.

Where you use these keywords can vary from platform to platform. On a website, keywords are added to page titles, meta descriptions, and page body text.
On Instagram, the most important location to add keywords is on the name line of your bio and in post hashtags.

The name line is the bold line at the top of your Instagram bio and when you go in to edit your profile, it's literally called "Name Line."

Ironically, the worst thing you can possibly put there is your name, or your business name.

When a customer is searching for your products or services, they don't actually know you yet. They won't be typing in your name. They don't know you exist yet.

The name line becomes very powerful when you use keywords here. Your visibility as a business on Instagram will increase exponentially when you have words about what you do and where you are listed in your name line.

And here's the kicker: you can't just compromise and put them in the rest of your bio down below. Because your actual written bio is not searchable. Not a single word of it. Just the name line!

The other critical location to capitalize on keywords is hashtags. Hashtags tell the Instagram search robot what your posts are about. It uses hashtags to find relevant posts for a users search. If you don't use hashtags, your posts are pretty much invisible to anyone but your followers.

Hashtags are most effective when posted in the actual caption right at the bottom. You can put some space between the caption and the hashtags just for readability's sake. Putting them in the first comment will not achieve the same results as putting them in the actual caption.

Focus your hashtags on the same types of keywords we discussed before: words and phrases that describe what you do and where you are located.

The amount of hashtags you're able to put in a post is typically 30, but that sometimes changes as the platform is updated. You might as well maximize on using them all.

The most efficient way to utilize hashtags is to create in advance three to five lists of 15-21 hashtags each. You can store these lists in your phone and just copy and paste them into your post captions.

Rotate through the lists to avoid utilizing the same set of identical hashtags over and over. When you use the exact same hashtag set every time, the algorithm flags it as spam and as a potential robot account, and will penalize your post performance for it.

Websites

When a person finds themself in need of a product or service, where do you think is the first place they go to look for a solution?

You guessed it: Google.

Consumers have been well trained to rely on Google as the

first method of searching for answers. This includes when they need information about where to purchase cake pops for a birthday party, who to hire to cater a wedding, or where to buy specialty custom cookies.

However, the majority of home bakers don't appear as a search result on Google.
Social media pages don't rank high as valuable results when you're searching on Google, so if you only market your baking business on social media pages you're missing an opportunity to be placed in front of potential customers.

Not all bakers choose to build a website- sometimes you can have plenty of success without it. However, due to the fact that not many bakers opt for a website, having one sets you apart. People often purchase from the first viable option they can find, so if you have a business website that pops up when they turn to the good old internet for answers, you're already ten steps ahead of the game!

I built my first website while I was still in school. I remember sitting in the back of the lecture hall, my professor rambling on about mass spectrometry, and I was busy creating a menu and an order form for my site.

That first iteration of my bakery website was very simple and quite amateur when it came to the design. But I bought it completely new customers from that website! People who I didn't even know!

I built the website using Wix, which is now my go-to web building platform thanks to it's easy drag-and-drop editing format. I've since used Wix to create at least half a dozen websites for various businesses.

When it comes to website design, simplicity is best. Use the style guide that you've already curated for your brand to guide you as you design each page. If you stick to your style guide, you'll be able to create a cohesive, consistent look throughout your website, and you won't waste precious time flipping through fonts and colors endlessly.

With a super customizable website builder like Wix, it's easy to fall into the trap of over-designing, but go back to the key points we covered about clarity and hold yourself to those. You want you fonts to be readable, your text to be minimal and to the point (people don't read!) and your overall style to be tastefully pleasing to the eye.

Keep the background of your website pages white for the most part. Colored backgrounds tend to be overbearing and distracting.

It can help to look at professional websites of similar businesses in your industry and get a feel for what is working and what you like about their designs.

Be sure to look at your website design not only as it's formatted for a desktop computer, but also a mobile layout version. Almost every site visitor you have will be looking at it on their phone. If your website is not formatted correctly for mobile, it's not going to do it's job. That's another reason that I've enjoyed building with Wix- it's super easy to toggle between the mobile and desktop layouts to make sure your design works in both (and I should note, this is a completely unsponsored, genuine opinion!)

Just like your social media pages, you want your website to be searchable. When people search for products and services on the internet, it's your job to do the footwork on the back end of the website so that search engines can tag your site as an inquiry result.

This is called SEO, or Search Engine Optimization. It's all about adding the right tags and keywords throughout your website and its pages in order to optimize their ability to appear as a search result. Search engines scan thousands of websites in less than a millisecond. The SEO you do on your website basically makes it readable to a search engine to quickly interpret what your website is about.

Most DIY website builders have a convenient simple SEO checklist built in as you design your site to guide you through the optimization process. You can also do additional research on how to push your SEO even further.

The first go-around with my own bakery website, I only utilized the free version of the site. This means that I didn't have an actual web address or domain that I owned and could customize. The Wix branding was also plastered permanently to my site and my domain name, unless I decided to upgrade to a yearly premium plan.

Eventually, I hit that point in my baking business journey that many bakers encounter: where you finally begin to take your business seriously and start to invest in growing it.

When I hit that point, I drafted a new 2.0 version of my website, fine tuning the design and the flow, and I took the leap to invest in that premium plan with a custom domain.

I remember the day so well. I went back and forth with my husband for hours trying to decide if we could afford to spend $180 to launch the site. That seemed like a huge amount of money to me at the time, and I wasn't sure if the investment would pay off.

But I took a deep breath, took a leap, and hit the purchase button.

In less than three weeks, I had made back my investment on the
website from the orders that it brought in. I have never looked back.

Other Digital Marketing Forms

Even beyond social media and websites, there are many creative ways to leverage existing online communities and platforms in order to spread the word about your baking business. You don't always have to spend the time building the audience and attracting people to your pages. It can be useful to explore paid advertising opportunities with entities and businesses that have essentially already collected the audience of potential customers for you.

Paid digital ads is one of these marketing forms. Essentially, Facebook or Instagram or whatever platform you choose to advertise you already has a collection of hundreds of thousands of users, and when you run a paid digital ad through their platform, you can very specifically target people who's demographic and psychographic information lines right up with that of your target customer.

You'll be able to see analytics on the ad performance, which can be incredibly informative on which ads are actually resonating with people. Digital ads can be a powerful tool for learning about your audience, but they often require a higher capital investment to really see drastic returns on your advertisements.

Another digital marketing lever you can pull is to make a guest appearance on a blog, social media page, or website that already reaches your target customers. This option involves a little bit of networking as well. You would want to spend some time to build a bit of relationship with the person or business you hope to be featured on. But it can be a powerful and genuine way to reach new potential clients.

One other easy digital marketing tool that you can always be working on is growing your mailing list.

When you're selling at a farmer's market, collect emails.

When you're handing out business cards at an event, collect emails.

When people order from you, collect their email!

The great advantage of a mailing list is you know your content lands in front of them. Any other digital platform, you're fighting against an algorithm to make sure people see what you post. Content gets lost easy in peoples' feeds, and sometimes just doesn't show up there at all. But when you have someone's email address and you send them an email, you know 100% that it's there in their inbox, and it has greater potential to be noticed.

Sending out occasional newsletters, promotions, and information about sales and products to customers' emails is a great way to keep them in the loop on your business. Never miss the chance to collect an email address!

The overall advantage of digital marketing is its potential to reach a lot more people, and oftentimes it's free if you utilize it well. A printed ad will only be seen by as many people as it can physically be in front of, while digital content has the power to reach incredibly large audiences.

At the same time, your content can get lost in a sea of information and visuals. There's so much going on; it can be trickier to stand out.

3. Network

Networking is simply connecting with other people in a symbiotic relationship of genuine support. There are three categories of networking that you can nurture and focus on:

- **Personal Network.** Reaching new customers through your own network of family members and friends. This is an important avenue when you're just starting your baking business because often friends and family are the first ones to take a chance on your new business and help you build your experience, your portfolio, and your credibility.

- **Professional Network.** Reaching new customers through professional relationships with other vendors in your industry, other businesses, and even other bakers. A professional network isn't about taking advantage of people. It's about collaborating together and supporting each other as business owners.

- **Customer Network.** Reaching new customers through previous or existing customers. This is incredibly powerful! Your actual customers are often connected with more people in your target market group, and a first hand recommendation or testimonial for your products and services from a human that has actual experienced them can be one of the greatest sources of business growth.

The key factor when it comes to networking is that it's so much more personal and more likely to convert into actual new customers.

Beyond receiving new customers, you also receive the benefit of just enjoying good company and support from others with shared industry experiences. These people get what it's like to be a business owner like you in this market! All my best friends are other bakers. We truly thrive off of each others' company.

Networking can feel intimidating and even discouraging at times. It does require consistent time and energy. You won't always make instant friends, relationships need cultivating. You also might not get on well with every business owner you meet, but always keep yourself polite, professional, and supportive.

4. Events

The last marketing channel I want to explore with you is events. Events are similar to networking in that you get to cultivate real, in-person connections with potential customers. Here's a few event opportunities to consider.

- **Farmer's Markets.** A market, typically held outdoors, featuring local artisans and farmers. The outdoor factor can make this channel an adventure logistically– most event hosts will not refund your booth fee in the case of inclement weather.

  In hot summer months, plan to keep products cool. I sold cake slices at a farmer's market in the peak of July heat once. I was pleasantly surprised at how well simple coolers with one ice pack each well maintained the temperature of my cakes.

  Wind is the other big one to be weary of during outdoor markets- it can come out of nowhere! I've spent too many markets standing at the corner of my booth, one hand holding the tent down, the other hand frantically trapping napkins blowing away. Always plan on how you'll keep the fort held down in case it gets gusty.

- **Expos.** These are larger events intended to showcase different types of vendors, businesses, products and services, that are typically related to each other in some way. In Utah, there is a yearly Sugar High Expo, which consists of hundreds of local bakeries and confectioners, and one admission ticket gets you access to treats and goodies from all of them! Other types of expos might include bridal expos, small business expos, and cake shows.

- **Sponsorship.** This involves donating money, time, or supplies to an event or cause in exchange for advertising space. You may or may not have a physical booth or table at the event.

- **Boutiques.** These are curated limited-time shopping events. They often center around a theme or holiday. Boutiques are hot spots for local artisans and craftsmen. Showing up as a sweet vendor often positions you as the concessions for the event— not bad to be the one-stop shop at the boutique for a little something sweet!

- **Pop-Up Shops.** You can host this yourself, or join a local one. I know many bakers who host their own simple pop-up shops on their own front porch. A friend of mine down the street, who is known in town for her cookies, has an actual mini fridge in her driveway that she consistently stocks with individually wrapped cookies and her Venmo posted on the door. People stop by all the time to buy her cookies!

One of the neat advantages to marketing your business at an event is that you're typically selling product there at the same time, so it's almost like a marketing opportunity that pays for itself.

However, it's important to note that the purpose of being a vendor or having a booth at an event is not always to turn a big profit from the small products you sell at the event itself. Events are about connecting with potential customers and fueling more orders for your business by making the community aware of your products and services.

Attend all events with this in mind: You're there to book new customers!

Talk to people, get them on your mailing list, get them to follow your social media pages, hand out business cards, help them book new orders with you right there on the spot.

Think ahead about how you'll keep connected to the people you meet at the event. The real power of participating in an event happens after the event, when people get back in touch with you. The potential to make a bit of money at the event itself is really just a nice side benefit.

How to Choose Your Marketing Channels

You absolutely do not have to utilize every marketing channel out there. In fact, trying to do so will most likely dilute the quality of your marketing efforts and spread your resources far too thin. You only have so much personal bandwidth and budget to put into your marketing, especially when you're wearing all the other hats of business owner, CFO, photographer, baker, and delivery driver. No need to overwhelm yourself by trying to run 5 different social media pages as well!

Where you choose to market and advertise your business depends completely upon who your target customer is. You want to show up in the places where they already hang out, whether that's in the physical world or the digital realm.

When I officially started my baking business in 2019, my very first marketing strategy was to participate in a farmer's market hosted at BYU, a nearby university. I knew that my target customer demographic was young couples getting engaged in Utah Valley, and I knew that the university was a hot spot for these types of people. But it can be tricky to market at a university– they're often very selective and closed to outside vendors. The weekly farmers market held in the BYU football stadium during the fall months was one of the only opportunities as an outside vendor to connect with the students– and I jumped on it!

My first farmer's market, Oct. 2019

I brought two types of cupcakes to sell (pumpkin spice and apple crisp), but I knew it wasn't really about the cupcake profit. I was there to book wedding clients. I brought a dummy cake that I actually decorated right there during the market. It seems crazy to try and decorate a cake outside, and I definitely didn't do anything too fancy, but it gave people a reason to come and talk to me. It helped me feel more approachable as a booth because I was present, but I wasn't just standing there staring them down. The market turned out to be a success for my brand new business! I booked two of my very first wedding clients from that event.

And then I did also have a little bit of cupcake revenue from the market, which more than offset the cost of being there in the first place. I call that a win-win!

Naturally, you would assume I went back to that market every year, since it had proven to be such a successful marketing channel that first year.

But I didn't.

It was actually an easy "no" for me as a business owner. My business had grown considerably, and I had begun to develop my own cake style with colorful, whimsical painted buttercream flowers. I was highly aware that the demographics of my target customer had changed. Young engaged couples at the university were low-budget when it came to wedding planning, which is okay! They just place higher value on elements other than a high-end, well-designed artistic cake. Those couples often ordered very simple, classic white cakes or naked cakes, less out of style preference and more out of budget restraints. It just wasn't a match anymore between those types of customers and my types of cakes. So I did not attend the farmer's market again, and I focused my efforts on new marketing channels.

The moral of the story is to know who your customers are and then be where they are!

As you begin to select your marketing channels, it's a good strategy to get started with no-cost channels that are quick and simple to utilize. Asking family and friends to share and spread the word about your business is easy and free.

Sending a DM to connect with a local venue or party planner is easy and free. There's a lot you can do to effectively get your business name out there without ever spending a dime.

Social media is one of the greatest gifts to small businesses. A free way to instantly connect and curate a relationship with just about any and all potential customers is a marketer's dream come true! Again, you don't need to build up a page and a following on every single platform. Pick the social media channels where your target customers are.

When I started my first cake business, I built my presence on Instagram. That is where my customers were. That is where people were finding me, so that is where I focused my efforts. Facebook was a dead end for my marketing. The target customer demographic that I wanted to reach were people who typically didn't even have Facebook accounts. To them, it was an outdated platform. So Instagram became my prime marketing channel, and it worked well! About half my order requests came from Instagram, the other half coming from my website.

Then after three years in business, I moved to a new city. Our new home was about a forty minute drive from our previous duplex, which didn't remove me completely away from the customer base that I had built. I could have continued just running my original business from my new city, and I do still take occasional orders that come through that first business. But as a business coach and a curious entrepreneur, I was intrigued by the thought of starting over from scratch.

Could I do it again?

Could I prove that success in business isn't about luck, but about mindset and applying solid business strategy?

So I set out to build an entirely new cake business in an entirely new city from the ground up.

The first eye-opening realization I had was that Instagram was not going to serve me as effectively as it previously had in connecting me to potential customers. As I had started to connect and build relationships with people in my new town, it was very apparent that everything in the community centers on real connection. It's all about who you know!

I switched up my marketing strategies to accommodate the characteristics of a new set of target customers. Instead of focusing efforts in the digital marketing world, I've focused on networking as my primary channel for reaching customers. I booked my very first order with my new business simply because I made a quick call to the library to ask about their upcoming Information Fair. After a friendly conversation with the head librarian, she ended up hiring me to make all the refreshments for the event– 300 mini cupcakes! So far, all of the new orders I've booked here have come to me through those networking channels.

Is paid advertising worth it?

I know many bakers who only utilize free marketing channels, mainly social media, and they thrive in orders. While free marketing opportunities in our technological world are amazing, it's important not to overlook paid marketing opportunities and how they can also be incredibly effective in connecting you with the right customers.

Whenever there's a higher potential for returns in business, it is typically accompanied by a heightened sense of risk. When you invest in paid marketing channels, you now have money on the line, and you want to know that it's going to come back to you.

Although it can feel scary and uncertain to spend money, I can't emphasize enough the importance of getting comfortable with investing in your baking business. It's ironic that as bakers, we'll complain all day and night about customers who make a stink about paying our high prices, yet when it comes to paying the price to grow our businesses, we embody that same attitude of resistance towards spending.

Money is not a limited resource. There's money all over the place. More will flow in. When you invest in the right opportunities, it can springboard your business into higher profit and success.

This doesn't mean that you just dish out dollars to any and all marketing channels that ask for your business. When evaluating a paid marketing opportunity (or honestly any marketing opportunity), these are the two factors to consider:

1. Will this channel/business/event/collaboration connect me with my actual target customer?

Don't just jump on any opportunity that someone presents you with. Ask questions about their audience, subscribers, and attendees. You need to know how well their audience aligns with your target customer.

When I first started an Instagram page for my business, I received a DM from a cake content page that shares other people's content on their feed. They had a large audience of over 200k followers, and they offered to repost one of my cakes to help bring people to my own page. The rate for a repost was only $17. And there I was, all bright-eyed and bushy-tailed with my new business on Instagram for the first time. I had no idea what I was doing and I was desperate for business growth. $17 didn't seem like too much to lose, so I went for it.

And I got a chunk of new followers! I got likes! The post did really well. But.....I didn't get any new customers from it. That is when it truly dawned on me what my purpose on social media was: Not to go viral. Not to have a "k" next to my following number. Not to connect with everyone. The whole point is to connect with my potential customers.

The audience demographics are the first thing to look at when evaluating a marketing opportunity.

2. How likely is it to make a return on my investment in this opportunity?

This question is answered with some simple math:

First, identify the initial outlay, or initial monetary investment, to participate in the opportunity? Let's say to have a booth at a bridal expo is $300.

Second, how many new customers would you need to acquire from this opportunity, not only to break even, but to generate a profit? If you're selling wedding cakes, let's say the cost of your average cake its $350. You would only need one customer to compensate for the cost of the booth fee, but it would be best to actually book 3-4 clients to make it a truly profitable investment, so we'll set that as your goal: To book 3-4 wedding clients from the event.

Based on past event data and analytics which can be provided to you by whoever manages the marketing channel, how likely is it for you to actually achieve those needed sales?

Perhaps the event manager lets you know that their foot traffic for last year's expo was about 1000 people, and they're aiming to increase that by 500 this year. How good are your chances that with 1500 people expected to come to the expo you can get four clients booked? You only need 0.2% of the event attendees to book with you. Those are pretty good odds!

You'll also want to consider booth placement, the expenses that you'll incur in addition to the booth fee, and whether there will be any other bakers with booths at the event. If there's going to be twenty bakers at the expo, booking clients might be a little more difficult, even with the high attendance. If you're going to give out samples, flyers, or utilize other supplies, be sure to include those expenses in your budget forecast for the event.

Once you've determined that the event is worth the investment of time and money, then focus on putting together the best presentation you can for it. Don't skimp! Make sure people remember you.

Are influencer collaborations worth it?

"Hi Hobble Creek Cake! I'm getting married in a few months, and have been looking for a baker for my cake. I couldn't find a good fit, until I came across your cakes and I'm just in love with them! I would love to invite you to be a part of an exclusive collaboration opportunity: My whole wedding is going to be showcased on my Instagram page, which has over 200k followers. In exchange for a cake, I would love to feature you on my page and highlight your beautiful work to my audience! Our wedding may even be featured in Brides Magazine.

Is this something you'd be interested in?"

Have you ever received a message like this? If you haven't, be prepared! Chances are you will. These requests can be well crafted with just the right placement of flattery to make you feel valued, important and lucky to be included.

Then they hit you with the payment deets: Exposure. Think of all the likes you'll get! All the new followers!

Don't let the sweet talk fool you. Whether it's an influencer wanting a wedding cake, a photographer needing a cake for a photoshoot, a request from a company or brand, what they're asking for is free cake and free labor, without any promise of guaranteed profit to you.

I fell into the trap one too many times myself. I've learned the hard way that even if the photoshoot ends up in a big wedding magazine, even if that influencer has 100k followers, exposure alone doesn't pay the bills. You don't get a paycheck from Instagram for likes and follows. You need to be savvy as a business owner in deciding whether or not a collaboration opportunity is a good fit for your time.

How To Evaluate Collaboration Opportunities

Not all collaboration opportunities are useless. Some may be beneficial to you, and there's strategic ways you can make things work in your favor.

Here's my top tips on how to evaluate a proposed collaboration, how to increase the possibility of a profitable return from your participation, and how to politely decline the opportunities that don't meet your criteria.

1. *Evaluate the Audience & Engagement Stats*

Dive right back into who you've defined as your target customer! Your target customer is typically tied to a *very specific local area* that you are capable of servicing. For you, it's not about getting your cake business in front of a large number of people. It's about getting your name in front of a very specific, local niche of people who can actually purchase from you.

Knowing *who* your work will be placed in front of is the first thing you'll want to evaluate about the opportunity. Request information regarding the audience from whomever is asking you for a cake collaboration.

Who do their posts reach? What's their age? Gender? Location? Does their audience actually engage with their content in meaningful ways?

Know who your own target customer is and make sure the collaboration audience aligns with that.

2. Consider Proposing A Different Collaboration Agreement

Even with the right audience, you still want to ensure a return on your investment. It's essential that you actually gain new paying customers as a result from the collaboration in order to truly profit from it. There's no guarantee that you'll get new orders from a simple tagged post or a social media shout-out.

Propose an arrangement with the influencer or brand that's more likely to result in profit for you. Maybe they don't get the cake for free right up front, but you can set up a referral agreement or promo code where they will receive some compensation for each of their referral customers who books with you in the future. This creates much higher incentive for the influencer or brand to spread the word about you and to do it well!

3. HAVE A CONTRACT!

All caps and underlined for a reason. Whatever the arrangement, make sure you have a written, signed contract with the person or company that defines exactly what is expected from both parties. Do not leave the terms open ended. You need to know exactly what to expect from them, and they should know exactly what to expect from you.

How do they intend to market your participation in the collaboration? How many times are they required to post about it and where will they post about it? What size of cake will you be providing? Do you get total creative freedom or do they get to have a say in the design? What kind of pictures will you get back from the collaboration? And what is the timeline for them to deliver on their end of the bargain?

Leaving things undefined is just asking to get burned, so make it official and be sure to get all the details in writing and signed!

4. How To Decline An Opportunity

Some opportunities just won't align with your goals or come with a promised return. In such cases, it's okay to politely decline and offer them your pricing options. If you have a message already typed up for these situations, it's a lot easier to say no- all you have to do is copy and paste!

Here's an example of a professional, polite message that you could send in order to decline a free cake request:

"Hello! Thank you for reaching out to me. I would love to be a part of this collaboration! At this time, I am only able to participate in paid collaboration opportunities. I've attached a copy of my collaboration rates below. If one of those options fits within the budget of your event, then I would love to work with you and further discuss the cake collaboration details! Please let me know what works best for you."

Remember my baker friend, you are playing a game for profit, not for a vanity number of likes and follows. Your time is valuable and precious, and you should be picky about how you spend it.

Lean In to the Unexpected

While selecting marketing channels for your business is a very intentional and strategic process, you can still leave room for serendipity! You can't predict where all of your orders will come from, or the real-time success of every marketing channel you explore. Leave yourself open to experiment, to gain data and feedback, to adjust, to take opportunities as they arise, and create your own opportunities when you need them.

The first boutique I ever sold at could've been considered a total flop. I brought hundreds of decorated cookies and sold maybe 35 total, having to pan off the rest through Facebook Marketplace at a discount price (which I should add, someone did buy them and I was incredibly grateful). It was also an outdoor boutique, and the wind unexpectedly picked up, causing the event to end early. At that moment, it felt like a disaster. But I took away many good lessons about how to run an outdoor booth, and also gained a very valuable and unforeseen new friendship that day with the owner of the venue where the boutique was hosted.

We enjoyed conversing about running our businesses and swapping stories from behind the scenes of our operations. Over the coming months, I participated in a few other events at her storefront. Then one day, a friend of hers needed a baker for a TV segment they were filming that week, and that is how I made my first ever appearance in front of a camera! The experience became a springboard for many more TV appearances and speaking opportunities, and I had my friendship with that venue owner to thank for passing the opportunity along to me in the first place.

Looking back, I don't regret being a part of that boutique, because I took away a lot more than just a few extra dollars.

Chapter 6

What If My Marketing Efforts Aren't Producing Results?

"You can't be everything to everyone, but you can be something to someone."
Drew Davis

Running a business comes with a lot of unknowns. There isn't a set in stone path or checklist to ensure success. You have to be ready to experiment, learn, pivot, and try again.

In his college years, Steve Jobs, the creator of Apple, randomly took a calligraphy class, to which he gives credit for founding the inspiration that led to his technological creations and success. Does this mean that if you go take a calligraphy class, you'll automatically be enabled to engineer the next great computer software? Not likely. I mean, heck though, if you're into that, go for it! I never say never!

It's not the exact steps on the path that Steve Jobs took which got him to success. His success came down to allowing for moments of creativity that broke the mold of the everyday routine. It was playing and experimenting in a field that excited him. It was the causal ambiguity of being in places that aligned with new thoughts and ideas that never could've been foreseen or predicted.

You have to bring your own creativity and enthusiasm to the table as you dive into marketing your baking business. The marketing channels you choose to use and the aspects of your brand identity that you decide to embody in business are ultimately your decision and your responsibility.

That's what makes this fun!

That's what allows you to grow as a business owner, and also just as a human. Learning how to communicate better, learning how to connect with others, learning how to better solve their problems is all a continuous process of growth and progress.

It's not about mimicking someone else's path– It's about building your own. Honestly, if business wasn't challenging it wouldn't be as exciting to participate in!

You may have moments when it seems that your marketing efforts aren't producing the results you're hoping for. These moments can be frustrating, and it's okay to recognize that. Recognizing moments of frustration and disappointment can actually be quite beneficial, because it helps signal to you that something is off and it's time to pivot or change direction. And in that moment lies a possibility for new opportunities and paths that you couldn't see before. Frustration and bad days aren't a sign for the universe that you need to quit. It's just a sign that it's time for a change.

When your marketing doesn't seem to be doing its job, here are a few of the factors you can stop to evaluate.

Revisit your product: Does it need improvements?

Taking a look at your product offerings is a simple place to start. It may be that you just need more time and practice to develop and polish your skills as a baker. We are all on a continual learning curve, getting better all the time. I believe in practicing, and practicing often. It was thanks to consistent practice that my own cake work got cleaner and more professional, and not to mention faster. It was thanks to practice that my signature style and cake design was born.

Doing an honest self-evaluation of your own product can be tricky. It may be helpful to enlist the opinions of good friends or colleagues you trust and who align closest with your target market analytics to give you product feedback. It's also important to make sure you get feedback from the right people. My sister once started a small business selling vegan baked goods. She would get discouraged after less than enthusiastic feedback from our family members, but none of them lived a vegan lifestyle. To them it didn't matter whether the treat was vegan or not. Their insights were not truly relevant because they weren't her target market.

Revisit your pricing: Does the perceived product value match the price?

Price sends a message to a customer about the value of your product.

We naturally and subconsciously interpret the meanings of prices all the time. It's important that your prices match the perceived value of your products in the minds of your customers.

Notice, I said the minds of your customers, and not your own mind. You will never value your products as highly as someone else because you make them! You can bake and create in a way that your customers can't, or just don't want to put in the time to do. To you, your products feel very accessible and commonplace because you make them often. But to someone else who places their time and efforts elsewhere, custom baked goods can be of great value.

If you're not getting the amount of orders that you want, it may be that you're still in the start-up stages of learning to bake and decorate. You're still improving your products to match the expected value of the customer.

Does this automatically mean you're obligated to charge less? No!

You are the highest authority when it comes to pricing in your business. Just because you're a beginner or have been operating less time than someone else doesn't mean you have to hold back your prices if the *value is already there*.

But if you're still easing into this whole baking and selling thing, and your comfort level squirms about your ability to actually deliver on an order, then you can start at a lower price with a plan to increase incrementally as you develop your own skills and experience.

Don't hold back on your pricing just because of fear. When it comes to money, it's easy to attach a lot of unnecessary emotions to it. Greed, selfishness, evil. I'm sure you've heard money or people with money labeled as one of those terms before.

The reason we make these associations isn't because money itself is bad. Money is a neutral resource that is neither good nor bad. It's just a tool to be used. Like a hammer lying on the ground. Someone could come along and pick up a hammer and do some seriously terrible things with it. Or you could come along and pick it up, and build something incredible and beautiful with it. It's not the hammer itself that's good or bad. It's the intentions and character of the user.

Money is the same.

In marketing, lowering the price seems like the easiest lever to pull in order to bring in more customers. However, it can be damaging to your brand and hard to recover from.

Having a price that is too low can actually cause you to lose customers, just as much as a price that's too high. Your price point speaks to different customer groups depending on what they value. Low price speaks to people who value cheap, easy, and cost saving, rather than quality, design, or taste.

If your prices are too low, then those are the customers you will continue to attract– the ones who want to nit-pick each line item while you bend over backwards to try and meet their extravagant requests on a budget just to win their business.

A higher price sends a completely opposite message.

While you'll lose the business of the low-end customers, you'll gain the attention of people who do place value on quality, design, and taste. To them, the purchase is more than just a product. It's an entire experience, a moment, and a vibe. They are ready and willing to pay for someone to execute their vision well. Those are the types of people who don't want the lowest price. They understand that lower price often implies lower quality, lower confidence and lower expertise. These customers can't take a gamble on that because their order matters to them so much.

I saw the reality of this back in 2019 when my newly formed cake business was just a few months old. My husband was accustomed to my constant rants about people not wanting to pay, but how I couldn't budge on the pricing and how it was always a constant battle to get people booked.

A few months into my business, I got a DM from a fellow baker in the area. She'd been in business way longer than I had, and I viewed her as one of the true pros in the industry. She was kind, but straightforward in telling me that I had priced my products way below their true value. My three tier cakes weren't even over $200. She said I had a good portfolio with clean work an could stand to raise my pricing quite a bit.

I took her message as an inspired nudge in the right direction and I raised my prices. And just a few months later I raised them again. And then a few months later raised them again.

I raised my prices four times just in that first year of business alone.

And do you know what happened?

The price-nit-picking customers were gone.

My husband noted to me one day, "I haven't heard you complain about customers not liking your prices in a while."

"That's because it doesn't happen anymore," was my reply.

The people who were looking for a bargain had just dropped out of the picture completely. Now the customers I was dealing with were serious inquiries. Orders were booked again and again without complaint.

Why? Because price sends a message.

On the flip side, you my have the right price set but your branding just needs a little makeover to help communicate the value of your products to match the asking price. Especially when it comes to your photos, upgrading your brand identity can help show your business and products in the best light, and be a better match for your pricing.

Revisit your target audience: Do you need to shift?

If you're struggling to get the orders you want, it might be a sign that you've got your target customer wrong. Revisit the demographics and psychographics that you brainstormed about your target customer: Do they truly align with the people who most need and benefit from your products and services? Do you have research, data, and evidence to back up the assumptions you've made about who your target customers are?

To really understand your target customer, you have to step back and get out of your own head. It's helpful to get outside perspectives about who your target customer might be.

Talk to people inside and outside your niche. If you're a wedding cake designer, you might have thought your target customer was a recently engaged woman between the ages of 27-35, but then you realize that in actuality who you should be targeting are the high-end wedding planners who bring the vendor connections to the bride.

That realization would completely shift how you approach your strategy in marketing.

If you're running a Valentine's Day sale and struggling to get orders, it might occur to you that you've been marketing to the women who would love to have your treats, and while they are the end consumer that you have mind, it's actually the boyfriends and husbands you need to get in front of and talk to. That would change everything about where and how you market for your sale.

Have you really expended your marketing efforts to the fullest?

You've got a lot going on as a business owner. It's easy to feel overwhelmed and to feel that you've done everything possible to get your name out there. It's easy to get stuck in the same circle of business habits, doing the same thing, but expecting different results. At the end of the day, you may feel like you've used every option available to market your business. The truth is, you've probably put a lot of time and effort into a few options, but I'd be willing to bet there's almost a hundred marketing strategies and avenues that you haven't yet explored!

At the end of this book is an entire list of 44 Creative Ideas to Market Your Baking Business. I've used many of these ideas to gain new orders in my own business. Take time to read through the list and see if it sparks a new idea of how and where you could market your business. Push yourself to try something outside of your normal go-to options– that will allow you to land in front of new people in new ways that you never saw before.

Tune in to the Market Trends

We live in a market that's constantly changing. Spending habits ebb and flow with the seasons. When you look at the data, predictable patterns often emerge around customers' spending habits.

A baker in mid-January might start to panic because no orders are coming in. Panic like that often induces business decisions made out of fear, which tend to be less-than-good decisions.

In reality, a mid-January lull in business probably has nothing to do with the quality of your products or your marketing efforts, and more to do with the fact that the holiday season just hit people hard, budget and energy wise.

They're giving it a month before they start making big purchases again. They're exhausted from the winter month festivities and they aren't ready to start planning more events yet.

Start to attune yourself and expect these trends in the market. It's not crisis mode. It's a great time to work on the back end of your business and fine tune your operations.

I consistently stop taking orders for a month or two out of the year here and there in order to work on the back end of my business. My baker friends have had a hard time understanding why I do this. Aren't I missing out? How can I afford to say "no" to so many order requests?

Actually, I can't afford to say "yes". I can't afford to keep going in exactly the same way without taking time to rest, regroup, and re-evaluate the direction I want to take my business in.

Taking time off from orders gives you time to stop flying by the seat of your pants and get intentional about your intentions. When you come back, the orders are still there. The customers are still there.

I took nine months off from my business in 2021 when I was pregnant with my second baby. I said "no" to literally hundreds of orders. But once I was recovered and ready to get back into business, I reopened shop and there were all the customers waiting to pour in! I easily fell back into step booking plenty of orders for the coming year.

The lesson here is to act out of belief, not fear.

Chapter 7

Infinite Possibilities!

"I dwell in possibility"
Emily Dickinson

....

Last year I adopted a new mantra for my life and my business:

God's love for you is infinite.
Your worth is infinite.
Your possibilities are infinite.

As we wrap up this incredible marketing deep dive that we've been on through these chapters, that is the message I want to leave with you my friend. I believe that you have a dream to bake and create for a reason. I know you have a purpose, because God doesn't make extras. He was intentional about creating you and the passion inside you to pursue this dream comes from the greatest love.

You don't have to run a successful business in order to validate your worth. I never tell anyone to charge what they're worth.

What the heck do people even mean when they say that???

Your worth is infinite and no one could afford your prices if you did that. You're worthy now. You're deserving now.

The story is actually the reverse: You don't have to reach a goal to be worthy. You reach your goals by embracing and believing in the immense worth you already hold right now, today. That is what propels positive action forward. That is what carries you through the ups and downs and challenges of business. Untie yourself from the hustle. You are everything you need to be right now.

You don't have to be a victim of circumstance. You don't have to suffer because of a lack of resources. The best thing about being in business is getting to write your own story, be your own boss, and create possibilities for yourself.

Don't wait for opportunities- make them!

No one came and told me it was my turn now to run a cake business. I just chose to lean full force into my dreams and my creativity to craft beautiful and delicious moments for people.

No one ever came to me and gave me permission to teach classes. I decided that I wanted to create that experience for people and I went out and figured out how to do it.

Nobody came along and said they would give me a chance to write this book. I just knew it was needed so I wrote and published it myself.

You have the same power inside of you to make things happen!

To put it bluntly, nobody is coming to save you.

You're going to save yourself.

By just being who you are and showing up to serve in this world.

I hope that everything you've learned from this book has helped you gain knowledge and perspective to push your business forward, upward, and onward.

I hope that you have success and that you keep the orders coming!

45 Creative Ideas to Market Your Baking Business

1. Send "postcards" to local businesses
I learned this from my husband in his illustration career. He literally sends postcards and posters to companies he hopes to work with as a way to get his contact information to them in a fun, physical, memorable form.

2. Put business cards in shops
Any shop that connects with the same customers as your target customers is a great place to leave some business cards! It doesn't hurt to bring samples for the managers and employees too, so they can give honest raving reviews for your work.

3. Be a preferred vendor
You can be a preferred vendor with other similar businesses in your industry, such as party and wedding planners, venues, photographers, dress shops, rental companies, etc. Sometimes businesses will require payment for you to become a preferred vendor, but often you can make real connections and become a preferred vendor just out of a true relationship with people.

4. Do a giveaway w/ other vendors
Connect with other vendors in your area and offer a giveaway package in exchange for audience contact information and to help increase local reach. Whether that's a follow, a post share, or an email, it can help connect you with new audiences that fit your target customer demographics.

5. Ask friends to share

Cash in on all those "I Owe Yous"! There's nothing wrong with a shameless request to friends and family to help get the word out about your business. You can message people personally or in a group. It's helpful to provide them with an image to use when sharing, or with a bit of guidance on what to say. Make sure they share a way to get in contact with you, whether that's a link to your page or an email address.

6. Customer referral program

Round up your most loyal and satisfied customers and offer them a reward for referrals they bring in.

7. Put a cake dummy in a shop

Ask a local bridal or florist shop if you could set up a dummy display cake to help showcase your work to and connect with their customers

8. Have a free sample day

Set up a little pop up table somewhere (make sure it's somewhere your target customers will be!) and hand out free samples. Remember to collect contact information!

9. Have a free consultation day

Use a bit of your marketing budget to host a free consultation day. Have a few slots available and invite couples to come and meet with you and try your cakes and talk designs.

10. Booth at an expo
Participate as a vendor at an expo. Expos are usually a collection of various businesses and vendors within a similar industry. They typically happen annually.

11. Booth at a market
Participate as a vendor at a market. Markets typically happen weekly, and are a great way to connect with the local community on a recurring basis.

12. Post on social media
An obvious one, but here's some tips:
1. Add key words about your products and location to the name line on your Instagram page. It's the only part of your bio that's searchable and helps connect you to customers searching for products and services like yours.
2. Use key words about your products and location in your hashtags. This is how social media search engines know what your post is about, and are able to connect it as a relevant result to customer searches.
3. Don't forget to share often on your personal pages as well as your business pages! Keep both your personal and professional networks in the loop.

13. Build a mailing list
Mailing lists are powerful tools because, unlike social media, the message lands without a doubt in their inbox. It allows you to prepare customers for upcoming sales, events, and product launches.

14. Bring treats to work

If you have a full-time or part-time job, practice baking and bring it to work with you! Make sure everyone sees your business information when they grab their treat by setting up business cards or some kind of visual to help them know who made it.

15. Send treat with family/friends to their work

Similar to bringing treats to your own work, but this way you connect with entirely different networks of people! Again, make sure everyone sees your business information when they grab their treat by setting up business cards or some kind of visual to help them know who made it.

16. Bring samples to bridal shops for the employees

If you're looking to get wedding orders, this can be HUGELY beneficial. Make sure those bridal shops know who you are, and make sure they have tried your products enough to rave endlessly about you to any customer who comes in!

17. Ad in local magazine

Experiment with buying ad space in a local magazine publication. Always check the audience and make sure it aligns with your target customers!

18. Partner with a venue for consultations

Offer to host a free cake or dessert bar tasting consultation for clients having consultations with a local venue. That might help elevate the whole experience for the clients and help them kill two birds with one stone.

19. Collaboration discount with other professional
Set up a collaboration referral discount with another professional in the industry. For example, if there's a party planner whose work you really like and whose customers are similar to your customers, suggest a deal where you'll give any of their booked customers 10% off if they'll give any of your booked customers 10% off.

20. Collaboration photoshoot
Get together with a photographer and other vendors and put on a mock wedding or party photoshoot in order to help each of you build your portfolios and experience. This can be a great way to network, build your portfolio, and advertise all at the same time!

21. Offer a free event planning & vendor guide
Make a list of your own preferred vendors and make it available to people. This helps provide them with free value before they've even ordered, and helps build trust and goodwill with clients.

22. Build a Website
I'm a big advocate for websites! When we're searching for products and services, 99% of the time we will go to Google first. Coming up in a Google search is rare in the home baking world, so if you can get your website to come up that puts you ten steps ahead!

23. List with third party site

There are many third party websites and companies who you can list with to connect with potential customers and clients. Wedding Wire and The Knot are examples of this. Essentially, they do the footwork to collect the audience for you, and then provide you with options, both free and paid, to get yourself in front of that audience.

24. Remember previous customers birthdays

How special would a customer feel if you reached out a month before their birthday to give them an early greeting and offer to make their cake again this year? All people want is to feel seen, and this would do the trick.

25. Make birthday cakes for friends and family

This is how most of us build our portfolios and experience in the beginning, and I still love it as a way to keep up my marketing and my skills.

26. Run a special or discount promotion

You can run a limited time special ("Book your cake today and get free delivery!") or a discount ("10% off all Mother's Day orders). This can help create urgency in the customers mind and get people booked faster. Be sure to outline clearly the applicable dates for the discount and the terms and conditions regarding it.

27. Promo on a fellow vendors page or email list

See if a fellow vendor would be willing to give you a specific shout on their social media page or in their weekly email, especially if you have any specific sales, promotions or events coming up

28. Connect with event & wedding planners
The power of connecting with people is huge! How do you do this? You just start making friends. You ask how you can support them. You send them referrals, you take them to lunch. Build a real relationship!

29. Connect with venues
Every venue in your area should know your business name. Again, be a real person! Support them first, and they'll support you.

30. Sponsor a local event
You can offer to sponsor a community event whether it's at a school, the library, or through the city. Maybe you could provide a raffle prize, or a goodie for swag bags in exchange for ad space in all the event materials.

31. Be a guest speaker at local schools
Lots of Home Ec. teachers and Foods teachers would probably absolutely love to have you come and speak to their classes! Be sure to bring something tangible that the kids can take home to their parents.

32. Join your local chamber of commerce
A chamber of commerce is typically a membership based group of local businesses that support each other and host educational events for improving business. It's a great way to network and gain community support.

33. Introduce yourself at city meeting
If your city council hosts weekly or monthly meetings that are open to public attendance, see if you can get on the agenda and introduce yourself. Don't forget to bring samples!

34. Post in local Facebook pages and introduction yourself
If it's allowed on your community page, take a moment to introduce yourself and your business to the group members.

35. Collect & share/publish your customer reviews
The power of customer reviews is real! Reach out to all your customers from the past year, thank them again for how their support and orders helped grow your business, and ask if they'll take a quick moment to leave you a review to help you grow even more.

36. Talk to people about your business!
Tell people!!! Don't be shy about it. It's not salesy, it's cool. It lets people get to know you and then they're able to support you when they get the chance.

37. Create a calendar for customers
Using your product photos, make a simple, nice calendar that you could hand out to customers at an event, or leave at shops like a business card. You can even put in the dates when your goodie sales will be so they'll have good notice.

38. Targeted Facebook ads
You can try a paid ad on Facebook to see if it helps you reach more of your customers. Experiment with your audience on a low budget first. Run two ads with different audience specifications for a day or two with just $20. See which one does the best, and then put more budget towards the better performing ad, while canceling the other.

39. Send referrals to other vendors
This helps build those real connections! Consciously look for opportunities to send customers to fellow vendors. They will thank you by sending customers to you too.

40. Teach a very basic free mini class

I've hosted little free classes at my local library. We had 70 people attend one. I just talked about the history of Minnehaha Cake and its relation to Henry Wadsworth Longfellow. I had people sign in and share their emails with me, which kept them in contact for upcoming classes and sales.

41. Make a VIP list

This is one of the most brilliant marketing moves I ever made in my business. People would constantly tell me to let them know when I had extras available. So I made a list of everyone and called them my VIP Cake Group. Whenever I had extras or even when I wanted to practice a design, I would send a push out to my VIP group and they would get first dibs on my extras at a good discount. It was a great way to get people trying my product, helped eliminate waste, and helped me make a little extra cash.

42. Host a sample night for event planners

Similar to hosting a free sample day for customers, but this time inviting event planners. Make it a nice classy evening for everyone to connect with each other and sample your products at the same time.

43. Visit local business, meet the owners and bring samples

This is a great way to connect with business owners outside your niche. We've talked about visiting bridal shops and party planners, but what about the local barber shop? Connect with the owner and ask if you can swing by to introduce yourself and bring them a little treat. Maybe bring extras for whatever customers are in the store at the time. Building connections is always a good idea.

44. Write a blog post for a blog that shares your target audience

If there's a local blog that connects with your target customers, ask if you can write an article for it.

45. Put up flyers on community bulletin boards

Good old fashioned bulletin boards around the community can still be a good way to get your business in front of fresh eyes.

About the author

Brette Hawks was studying Food Science at BYU in Provo, Utah when she stumbled into the business world. In hopes of ditching a few chemistry classes, she opted for the industry management major track, which allowed her to enroll in classes such as entrepreneurship, marketing & strategy, finance, economics, and accounting. She quickly fell in love with business, and when she combined it with her life-long love of baking, it was the perfect springboard into launching her own wedding cake business!

It's always easy to look at how much someone has accomplished and assume it happened over night. Rest assured that this was not Brette's story!

After 3 years of trial and error, many late night orders, never-ending dishes, and LOTS of practice, Brette grew her little home-based cake venture, named Hobble Creek Cake Co. for the local beloved canyon area, into a thriving, reputable designer wedding cake business that has been featured by brands such as Wilton, Cake Masters, and American Cake Decorating Magazine.

Brette's goal now as a business coach for bakers is to be the resource she wish she'd had when she started out!

When she's not baking, she's playing with her two little rascally boys, out for a run, or enjoying a late night movie with her husband Nate.

Congratulations!

You now have all the tools you need to master marketing. That's a huge step in the right direction my friend, and I am so excited for the journey that you are on!

My goal is to be your ultimate resource and guide through every step in the process of growing your baking business.

Don't forget to keep in mind all the ingredients in the recipe for success:

1. Your plan
2. Your product
3. Your pricing
4. Your marketing strategy
5. Your customer service
6. Your financial management

You can visit www.outofhomebaker.com to enroll in my full online business building program the Business School for Bakers, or browse resources by individual topics.

Together we'll bake it happen!

Made in the USA
Monee, IL
30 July 2023